The Continuation War 1941–44

Soviet Soldier
VERSUS
Finnish Soldier

David Campbell

Illustrated by Johnny Shumate

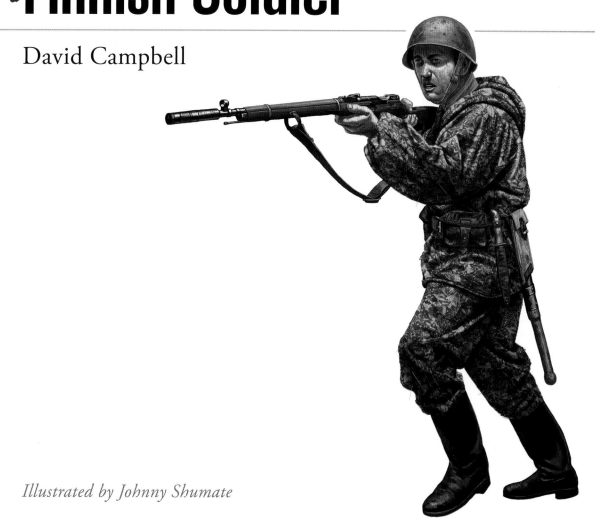

OSPREY PUBLISHING
Bloomsbury Publishing Plc
Kemp House, Chawley Park, Cumnor Hill, Oxford OX2 9PH, UK
1385 Broadway, 5th Floor, New York, NY 10018, USA
E-mail: info@ospreypublishing.com
www.ospreypublishing.com

OSPREY is a trademark of Osprey Publishing Ltd

First published in Great Britain in 2020

© Osprey Publishing Ltd, 2020

A catalogue record for this book is available from the British Library.

ISBN: PB 9781472838308; eBook 9781472838315;
ePDF 9781472838285; XML 9781472838292

20 21 22 23 24   10 9 8 7 6 5 4 3 2 1

Maps by www.bounford.com
Index by Rob Munro
Typeset by PDQ Digital Media Solutions, Bungay, UK
Printed and bound in Italy by Printer Trento Srl.

Osprey Publishing supports the Woodland Trust, the UK's leading
woodland conservation charity.

Dedication
For Tristan and Alison, fellow veterans of the Leicester campaign.

Acknowledgements
I would like to thank the Finnish military picture archive SA-kuva
(http://sa-kuva.fi/), a splendid resource that has made thousands of
images from the Winter, Continuation and Lapland wars available for
anyone to view and download – a significant aid in the research and
composition of a book such as this. I would also like to pay particular
regard to several online resources that are every bit as important as the
more traditional sources one finds in a bibliography: www.mosinnagant.
net contains much first-class information on Soviet and Finnish small
arms of the period; http://militera.lib.ru is a valuable repository of
many Russian-language wartime accounts that would otherwise be
extremely difficult to obtain; and www.jaegerplatoon.net is the single
best available English-language resource concerning the weapons,
uniforms and organization of the Finnish armed forces, both online and
in print – anybody wishing to delve deeper would be well advised to start
there. Thanks are also due to Graham Campbell for his contributions
to my interminable library infrastructure project; to David Greentree
for encouraging profitable lines of research regarding Soviet armoured
vehicles; to Geoff Banks and his ongoing efforts to become a cautionary
tale; and to Nick Reynolds who makes sense of all the pieces.

To find out more about our authors and books visit
www.ospreypublishing.com. Here you will find extracts, author
interviews, details of forthcoming events and the option to sign up for
our newsletter.

Ranks

US (1941)	Finnish	Soviet*
General of the Army	*Generalfeldmarschall*	*Marshal Sovetskogo Soyuza* (Marshal)
General	*Sotamarsalkka*	*General Armii* (Army General)
Lieutenant General	*Kenraali*	*General-polkóvnik*
Major General	*Kenraaliluutnantti*	*General-leytenant*
Brigadier General	*Kenraalimajuri*	*General-mayór*
Colonel	*Eversti*	*Polkóvnik*
Lieutenant Colonel	*Everstiluutnantti*	*Podpolkóvnik*
Major	*Majuri*	*Mayór*
Captain	*Kapteeni*	*Kapitán*
1st Lieutenant	*Yliluutnantti*	*Stárshiy Leytenánt* (Senior Lieutenant)
n/a	n/a	*Leytenánt* (Lieutenant)
2nd Lieutenant	*Vänrikki*	*Mládshiy Leytenánt* (Junior Lieutenant)
Sergeant Major	*Vääpeli, Sotilasmestari*	*Starshiná*
Staff Sergeant	*Ylikersantti*	*Stárshiy Serzhánt* (Senior Sergeant)
Sergeant	*Kersantti*	*Serzhánt* (Sergeant)
n/a	n/a	*Mládshiy Serzhánt* (Junior Sergeant)
Corporal	*Alikersantti*	n/a
Lance Corporal	*Korpraali*	*Yefréytor* (Senior Private)
Private	*Sotamies/Jääkäri*	*Krasnoarmeyets* (Red Army man)

* Junior officers (*Mládshiy Leytenánt* to *Kapitán*) in rifle divisions would have an accompanying political officer, a Politruk, and senior officers (up to
army commanders) a commissar.

CONTENTS

Introduction

Finland's defence of its borders during what became known as the Winter War (November 1939–March 1940) was heroic by any measure, garnering the small country much international sympathy and equal measures of opprobrium for Stalin and humiliation for the Red Army. Despite the gallant resistance of the Finns and the Pyrrhic nature of the Soviet victory, however, a victory it was; Finland lost nearly 10 per cent of its territory, including the port city of Viipuri and the Karelian Isthmus, forcing the relocation of 12 per cent of the country's population to behind the newly drawn border. Undoubtedly the strength of Finnish resistance stopped the outcome from being very much worse, but that was cold comfort in the face of their brutal neighbour's gains. The bad faith and open aggression that characterized the Soviet approach to Finland in the run-up to war had not disappeared with that conflict's conclusion; there was little doubt that Stalin's long-term view of a peaceful Baltic did not involve an independent Finland, with the Soviet Union strong-arming potential diplomatic and military allies to refuse any help for the Finns while he annexed the Baltic states – Lithuania, Latvia and Estonia – on 17 June 1940. The most obvious potential ally, Sweden, prevaricated in the face of Soviet belligerence, opting to remain neutral.

Germany's invasions of Denmark and Norway on 9 April 1940 increased the Finnish sense that they were trapped between the manoeuvrings of two vast powers, and indeed German planning for Operation *Barbarossa* (the invasion of the Soviet Union) involved the Finns, though at this stage they had no knowledge of their mooted part in Hitler's grand scheme. The first concrete link between Finland and Germany came with the former's agreement on 12 September 1940 to allow free passage of German equipment and troops from its bases in Norway, but it also offered the Finns a desperately needed avenue to re-arm; from the date of the agreement to June 1941, 53 fighter aircraft, 185 pieces of field artillery, 112 anti-aircraft guns, 300 anti-

tank guns and 150,000 ant-tank mines were delivered from Germany to the Finns (Tillotson 1996: 189).

Despite increased tensions between Moscow and Berlin the official Finnish position was one of neutrality, the country only prepared to go to war if it were attacked once again. Even so, Field Marshal Carl Gustaf Emil Mannerheim, head of the Finnish Army and the most significant figure in the Finnish government, quietly developed contingencies for mobilization in the event of a German war with the Soviet Union. By 25 May 1941 Germany's plans were becoming increasingly obvious, as was the diplomatic pressure Berlin was exerting on the Finns to fall into line; the German plan for a combined assault with the Finns on Petsamo and Murmansk, Operation *Silberfuchs* ('Silver Fox'), was shared with the Finnish high command, as were Hitler's broader intentions towards the rest of the Soviet Union. Though he viewed the German leadership with contempt, Mannerheim had confidence in the strength and skill of the German armed forces, believing them likely able to defeat the Red Army; in such a circumstance he saw an opportunity to retake the Finnish lands seized by Stalin in 1940, thus regaining all their economic and defensive value for the nation. Finland would continue to insist on its neutrality, though it was clear that in the event of a German attack on the Soviet Union the Red Army, which already saw the Finns as being in thrall to the Germans, would strike out and give Mannerheim just cause to join the war. And so it proved.

The German hammer blow that was Operation *Barbarossa* struck on the morning of 22 June 1941 and included sorties by Luftwaffe aircraft that used Finnish airfields on their return legs, leading to Soviet aerial bombing raids against all major Finnish cities and industrial centres on 25 June. A few days later the first Finnish reconnaissance units crossed back into Karelia, vanguard of a force that would drive the Soviets before them and eventually

ABOVE RIGHT
Harlu, 26 July 1944: a Finnish soldier lights a cigarette as he waits to be interviewed on Finnish radio about the battles he had been involved in north-east of Lake Ladoga. He wears the m/36 field cap and lightweight summer tunic and carries a Suomi KP/-31 submachine gun. Pouches for the KP/-31's 70-round ammunition drum magazines were non-existent, so the latter were usually carried attached to the belt by improvised wire hooks or string, or stowed in the soldier's pack (each submachine-gunner was supposed to be issued with five drum magazines or seven 50-round box magazines). Note the field dressing hanging from his right hip. (SA-kuva 156258)

The losses suffered by Finland as a result of the Winter War (November 1939–March 1940) were substantial. As well as over 25,000 dead the country was forced to concede nearly 26,000km of territory in Karelia (including Käkisalmi, Sortavala and Viipuri, Finland's second-largest city), several islands in the Gulf of Finland including Suursaari, the lands of the Salla region on the central front, and Kalastajasaarento (the Rybachiy Peninsula) in the far north. In addition, the Soviets demanded the right to lease the harbour at Hanko on the southernmost tip of the country (less than 130km from Finland's capital city, Helsinki) for 50 years, a situation that, when taken with the loss of Viipuri and Suursaari Island, promised unpleasant Soviet naval influence in the Gulf of Finland for some time to come. The campaign of 1941 drove the Soviets out of their conquered lands and back deep into traditional Russian territory, but instead of a clean victory the Finns found themselves engaged in several years of static trench warfare. By the time of the Soviet resurgence in June 1944, the Finns found themselves fighting all along their new borderlands, though as in 1939 it was the Red Army's attack on the Karelian Isthmus that was most serious. With a heavily forested landscape dotted with swamps, numerous lakes and cut through with rivers, the open areas of the Karelian Isthmus are often rugged and rock-strewn, making it a difficult environment for a military campaign, especially one that relies on armoured and mechanized forces. Finnish defences were concentrated along the Main Line, the VT-Line (Vammelsuu–Taipale), the VKT-Line (Viipuri–Kuparsaari–Taipale) and finally the Salpa Line.

cut off Leningrad's northern approaches. Finland's reclamation of its territory was succeeded by 2½ years of static trench warfare, the border remaining unchanged until the turning tide began to approach once more. The 872-day siege of Leningrad by German forces was finally broken on 27 January 1944, and with the German armies engaged in a fighting retreat all along the Eastern Front it was only a matter of time before Stalin's spreading empire turned its attention back to Karelia and its insolent occupiers. As the summer of 1944 approached Finland braced itself for its third major campaign against the Red Army in four-and-a-half years. As in 1939, the objective for the Finns would not be so much to win as to survive.

Finnish soldiers built this improvised sled to carry food to their comrades at the front, 29 November 1941. Counter-intuitively, supply could be more of a problem in the summer months than during the winter; snow allowed the use of skis, as well as the adaptation of frozen lakes into ice roads. During the summer months the densely forested, lake- and river-dotted land of East Karelia meant that lines of communication were heavily reliant on existing roadways. The extremely low level of mechanization within the Finnish Army meant that draught animals were a necessity in keeping the front well-supplied. (Bettmann/Getty Images)

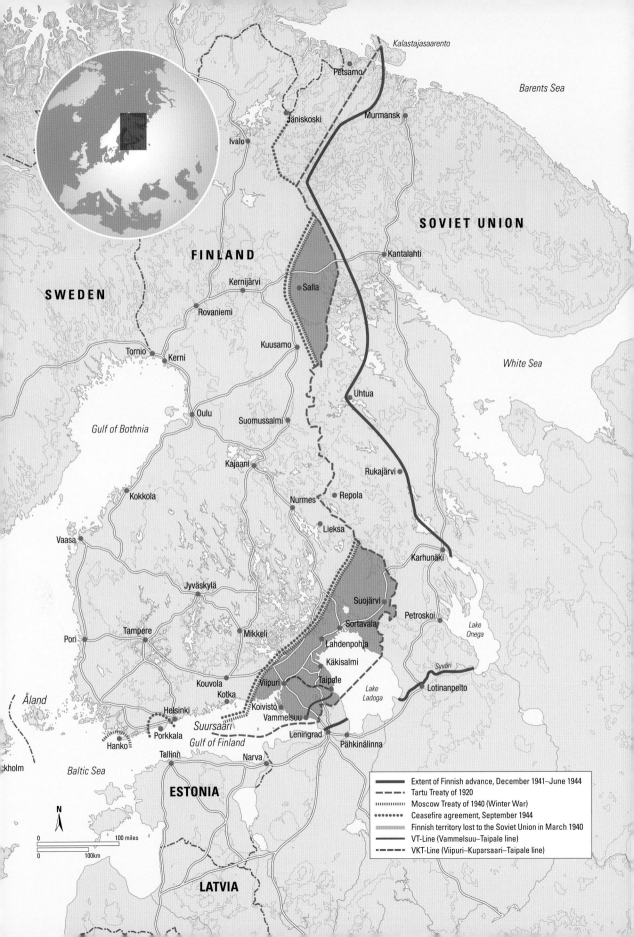

Kalastajasaarento

Barents Sea

Petsamo

Murmansk

Jäniskoski

Ivalo

SOVIET UNION

FINLAND

Kantalahti

Kernijärvi

Salla

SWEDEN

Rovaniemi

Kuusamo

Tornio   Kerni

White Sea

Uhtua

Oulu   Suomussalmi

Gulf of Bothnia

Kajaani

Rukajärvi

Kokkola

Nurmes   Repola

Vaasa

Lieksa

Karhunäki

Jyväskylä

Suojärvi

Pori   Tampere   Sortavala   Petroskoi   *Lake Onega*

Mikkeli

Lahdenpohja

Käkisalmi

Syväri

Kouvola   Viipuri   Taipale   Lotinanpelto

Kotka   *Lake Ladoga*

Helsinki   Koivisto

Åland   Vammelsuu

Porkkala   *Suursaari*   Leningrad

Hanko   Pähkinälinna

Tallinn

Gulf of Finland

Narva

ckholm

Baltic Sea

ESTONIA

N

0   100 miles

0   100km

▬▬▬▬	Extent of Finnish advance, December 1941–June 1944
▬ ▬ ▬	Tartu Treaty of 1920
┊┊┊┊┊	Moscow Treaty of 1940 (Winter War)
●●●●●	Ceasefire agreement, September 1944
●●●●●	Finnish territory lost to the Soviet Union in March 1940
▬▬▬▬	VT-Line (Vammelsuu–Taipale line)
▬ ▪ ▬	VKT-Line (Viipuri–Kuparsaari–Taipale line)

LATVIA

The Opposing Sides

ORIGINS

Soviet

At the outset of war the organization of Red Army rifle divisions was in a state of flux. The vicious lessons of the Winter War had shown that the pre-war 18,841-man division (with its 15-man rifle squads) was too big, and that the submachine gun (SMG) was a more important weapon in infantry combat than had previously been appreciated. The new Table of Organization and Equipment (TO&E) of April 1941 called for a reduced rifle division of 14,483 men with rifle squads of 11 men: a squad leader, a two-man light-machine-gun (LMG) team armed with a 7.62×54mmR DP, two men armed with 7.62×25mm PPD-40 or (later) 7.62×25mm PPSh-41 SMGs, and the remaining six men all carrying 7.62×54mmR SVT-40 gas-operated semi-automatic rifles; four such squads and a four-man 50mm mortar team would constitute a platoon.

The sudden plunge into full-throated war three months later on 22 June meant that such changes were only implemented haphazardly at best; not only were the rifle divisions faced with more pressing issues than the niceties of platoon organization, the Soviet state was nowhere near being able to equip the new rifle squads with the SMGs and semi-automatic rifles that were required – a situation that would not change substantially for many months. The 7.62×54mmR Mosin-Nagant M91/30 bolt-action rifle would remain the most ubiquitous weapon of the Soviet rifleman until the end of the war. As far as the larger elements of the rifle division were concerned, its structure remained more or less unchanged from earlier iterations, in other words unwieldy and overly complex; but the savage attrition of 1941 and the slow improvement in arms manufacturing and combined-arms tactics would see significant changes by the time of the 1944 campaign.

The desperate years of 1941 and 1942 had necessitated new rifle divisions being raised at a dizzying rate to replace those destroyed in combat, resulting in a series of haphazard changes to divisional organization and levels of manning, often only tangentially related to the reality that such units faced on the front line; by 29 July 1941 official rifle division strength had dropped to 10,859 men, with further changes in December 1941, as well as March, July and December 1942, by which time a rifle division was supposed to contain 9,435 men – half the strength of the Winter War rifle divisions. This instability led to a conscious attempt to regularize the TO&Es of rifle units, as well as bringing back the 'Guards' from the Imperial Russian Army. The decision to raise the first Guards rifle divisions (initially in Leningrad in July 1941 and officially by the Stavka (*Stavka Glavnogo Komandovaniya*, 'Main Command of the Armed Forces of the USSR') in September 1941) was driven by the need to recognize reliable units – those that had withstood the summer onslaught and maintained their offensive spirit – as well as bolster morale in the battered Red Army more generally, even if it meant recourse to an old imperialist title. Rifle divisions that had proved to be competent, reliable and combat-worthy were converted into Guards rifle divisions, with the newly redesignated formations being grouped into Guards rifle corps from 27 September 1941, even though the rifle corps headquarters for regular rifle divisions had been disbanded on 15 July 1941.

With the situation more stable in late 1942–43, the Stavka's emphasis shifted from raising fresh rifle divisions to one of nurturing existing forces, though this was driven in part by the fact that the pool of available manpower had been steadily shrinking since the catastrophic losses of 1941, resulting in the new 'reduced strength' TO&E of 22 August 1943. Each rifle platoon now had three 11-man rifle squads instead of four, with regimental strength overall falling from 2,443 men to 2,017 men and rifle divisions being 9,380 men strong. By the summer of 1944, continuing shortages resulted in a series

What seems to be the greater part of a platoon of Soviet infantry photographed as they leap from the T-34-85 medium tank that has carried them into battle. Soviet *tankodesantniki* ('tank descenders') were one of the informal innovations of the mid-war years that developed into an effective combined-arms tactic, allowing armoured units to enjoy ready infantry protection from enemy soldiers and light anti-tank weapons during their advance. Note that all the *tankodesantniki* are armed with PPSh-41, PPS-43, and at least one captured MP 40 submachine guns. (From the fonds of the RGAKFD in Krasnogorsk via Stavka)

The *razvedchik* ('scout') is advancing aggressively, with his rifle – the sniper's version of the 7.62×54mmR Mosin-Nagant M91/30 – at the ready. His clothes and equipment show the hard wear they have endured in the last few days, but his rifle is clean and well-cared for. In his reconnaissance role it is necessary to be able to move fast, so his equipment has been kept to the bare minimum, no more than what his belt can comfortably accommodate. His two-piece 'leaf'-pattern MKK camouflage overalls (*maskirovochnyi kamuflirovannyi kostium*, 'deceptive camouflage suit') are loose and light enough to be worn over his M43 summer field uniform without hindering his freedom of movement.

Weapons, dress and equipment

His main weapon is a Mosin-Nagant M91/30 bolt-action sniping rifle (**1**), but here he has removed the 3.5× PU sight and has instead fitted his weapon with a Bramit suppressor (**2**) attached to the muzzle. Over 60,000 Bramit suppressors were produced during the war (Chumak 2011: 74), with the majority being issued to reconnaissance units and partisans, as well as other specialized troops that could benefit from such a tool.

He wears an SSh-40 helmet (**3**) and 'leaf'-pattern MKK camouflage suit (**4**) over the top of his M43 summer field uniform. First issued in late 1940 or early 1941, the new pattern was, like the 1938 'amoeba'-pattern camouflage overalls and suits, mainly the preserve of reconnaissance forces, snipers, engineers and other specialists, and would see service throughout and well after the war. Weighing around 1kg, the 'leaf'-pattern MKK was produced in several colour variations (the grey-brown shown here as well as a brighter green version), and usually came with a hood large enough

to fit over a helmet together with a mesh face-mask. It was made from 100 per cent cotton, dried out quickly, and could be pulled on in under a minute.

His equipment consists of a plain belt, a 1941-pattern SVT/ Mosin cartridge pouch (**5**) that holds four five-round stripper clips. The Bramit required specialized subsonic ammunition, with the standard 7.62×54mmR cartridge adapted to use a smaller powder charge (0.8g instead of the usual 3.6g) which would propel the standard 9.6g bullet at a maximum of 260m/sec. This also resulted in a much-reduced range of 300m at most, with shots taken at 150–200m being the norm. Brass ammunition was marked with green varnish on the bullet and the base of the round, with later steel-cased cartridges sporting bullets (or the whole cartridge) varnished in black (Ponomarev 2010: 27). The soldier also carries a canteen (**6**), an entrenching tool (**7**) and a fighting knife (**8**).

of emergency TO&Es that front commanders had authority to employ, thus ensuring that even severely depleted units could remain on the front line; an intermediate rifle division could contain 7,189 men, down to the smallest option of 4,400 men (Zaloga & Ness 2009: 30–32). By 1944 a typical Guards rifle division was supposed to have 9,680 men, but actual strength was usually only 75–80 per cent of this figure at best; each of the rifle division's three rifle regiments now included two dedicated SMG companies of 100 men each, as well as the usual mortar, artillery and anti-tank companies. By December 1943 each rifle division was supposed to receive new 76mm guns to replace the underpowered 45mm M1937 guns in its anti-tank battalion, though precedence went to dedicated anti-tank formations, followed by mechanized units and then elite formations such as the Guards rifle divisions. From May 1944 individual Guards rifle divisions began replacing their 76mm anti-tank gun battalions with SU-76 battalions (12 76mm SU-76 self-propelled guns in three batteries), even though the official change was not authorized until December of that year.

Finnish

At the outset of the Continuation War (June 1941–September 1944) the Finnish Army consisted of 16 infantry divisions, two *Jäger* brigades and a *Ratsuväkiprikaati* ('cavalry brigade'). The roots of the Finnish Army came from the Königlich-Preußischen Jäger-Bataillon Nr. 27 (Royal Prussian Jäger Battalion 27), a German unit of World War I that was made up of Finnish volunteers whose veterans would go on to play a decisive role in the Finnish Civil War (January–May 1918) and the subsequent establishment of the national army. The experience of the officers who had come through such an education found its way into most aspects of Finnish planning, strategy and

A fine study of a Finnish soldier taken at the Vuosalmi Bridge Headquarters, 24 July 1944. He is armed with an older-model Suomi KP/-31 SMG fitted with the 50-round 'coffin' magazine (as opposed to the more common 70-round drum), and wears a distinctive German M18 helmet, one of the most common types in Finnish use during both the Winter and Continuation wars. The 50-round magazine was originally a Swedish design, manufactured under licence in Finland between 1941 and 1943; it would prove far too susceptible to damage in the field, and required a separate loading tool to boot, making it a far less popular option than the reliable 70-round drum. (SA-kuva 158795)

tactics, proving its worth in the hard fighting of the Winter War. The Finnish Army had proven itself to be effective, resilient and well-trained, but there were obvious problems in the lack of heavy equipment and the overall shortage of manpower when cast against the Soviet Union. Despite improvements in small arms, artillery guns and armour the size of the fully mobilized Finnish Army – 630,000 men and women (16 per cent of the population) at the start of Operation *Barbarossa* on 22 June 1941 – did not grow appreciably after 1941, though expenditure continued to rise from 45 per cent of the national budget in 1940 up to a crippling 70 per cent during the summer of 1944 (Johansen 2016: 222).

In addition, the experience of fighting the Red Army provoked changes to the structure of Finnish Army units, most importantly the blending of an infantry platoon's two light-machine-gun and two rifle squads into four rifle squads, each of which had a squad leader, a light-machine-gunner (armed with a 7.62×53mmR Lahti-Saloranta m/26 or captured Soviet DPs), a submachine-gunner (Suomi KP/-31) and six riflemen (7.62×53mmR m/28-30 bolt-action rifles). As the Continuation War progressed the rifle squad would see an increase in submachine-gunners, substituting for one and eventually two of its riflemen, as well as one of the remaining riflemen taking on the role of sniper or (due to the lack of suitable weapons and telescopic sights) dedicated marksman armed with a 7.62×53mmR m/39 'Ukko-Pekka' bolt-action rifle.

During the Winter War the Finnish artillery arm had mostly been notable for its paucity, while armour had been effectively non-existent. Captured Soviet artillery guns helped to bolster the Finnish Army's small artillery park, largely made up mostly from a mixture of old French and Imperial Russian pieces that dated from World War I back to the late 19th century, as did purchases from the likes of Sweden (12 105mm K/34 heavy field guns), France (48 75mm K/97 light field guns) and Germany (24 120mm K/78-31 and 12 155mm K/17 heavy field guns). Despite such acquisitions and the Finnish artillery arm's effectiveness in deploying such a bewildering variety of field guns, it was never anything like a match for the Soviet artillery of 1944.

In terms of tanks the Finnish Army's Winter War *Panssarijääkäripataljoona* ('armoured battalion'), a mixture of obsolescent British and French tanks supplemented with captured Soviet vehicles, served successfully in the 1941 campaign of the Continuation War and was expanded into a *Panssariprikaati* ('armoured brigade') on 9 March 1942, and then into a *Panssaridivisioona* ('armoured division') on 28 June of that same year. The new armoured division consisted of a *Panssariprikaati* ('armoured brigade') with two battalions of mostly captured Soviet tanks, a *Rynnäkkötykkipataljoona* ('assault-gun battalion') that from late 1943 was equipped with StuG III assault guns bought from Germany, and a *Jääkäriprikaati* (*Jäger* Brigade) which would prove to be a vital asset in the battles at Kuuterselkä and Tali–Ihantala during the Soviet attacks of June 1944.

The *Jääkärit* (Jäger) had their origins in the Finnish Civil War, but at that stage there was little distinction between them and any other infantry formation. By the 1930s, however, the *Jääkärit* had developed into a light-infantry striking force mounted on skis or bicycles depending on the

The *korpraali* (lance corporal) has had a hard day; his uniform and equipment, like those of almost all of his comrades, show the dirt and wear that accumulate all too quickly when fighting on the front lines. He wears only a simple badge of rank, faded collar tabs that mark him out as a lance corporal. The m/36 tunic was originally meant to have rank markings on the shoulder straps which also sported coloured piping to show the branch of service, but that practice was discontinued in 1941, all officers and men henceforward supposed to use coloured collar tabs to show their branch and rank, though shortages meant that this was hardly a universal practice.

Weapons, dress and equipment

His primary weapon is a 7.62×25mm PPS-43 SMG (**1**), a much-valued trophy captured from the enemy. Weighing only 3.04kg, the PPS-43 was an excellent weapon: rugged as well as simple to operate and maintain, it used reliable and sturdy magazines (one of the great failings of the PPSh-41 SMG) and would later be copied by the Finns in the shape of the 9×19mm m/44. Like most of his compatriots, this soldier started using the PPS-43 the moment he captured it, such weapons usually only being passed back to the ordnance branch when they broke or ran out of ammunition.

He wears an m/36 cap (**2**), a popular item with both officers and men that was affectionately known as the *verikauha* ('blood scoop'), its blue-and-white cockade marking him out as an NCO or enlisted man (officers had a red enamel pin sporting a rampant lion in gold). His uniform is the stone-grey m/36 summer tunic (**3**) and trousers, with plain jackboots. He is equipped with an m/22 belt (**4**), a captured three-cell canvas pouch for his PPS-43's 35-round magazines (**5**), an m/40 bread bag (**6**), a canteen (**7**) copied from the German M15/17 pattern flask, a *puukko* knife in a hand-tooled sheath (**8**) and a *varsikranaatti* ('stick grenade') m/32 stuffed in his belt (**9**). The m/32 was slightly smaller and lighter than the German M24 *Stielhandgranate*, but retained the belt clip common from World War I models. It was superseded by the almost identical *varsikranaatti* m/41, which finally omitted the clip.

season; there were six *Jääkäripataljoonaat* (JP, '*Jäger* battalions') that were brigaded before the start of the Continuation War (1. Jääkäriprikaati and 2. Jääkäriprikaati, the latter abolished in the spring of 1942), intended to act as a highly mobile elite striking force in support of the main Finnish Army attack on the Karelian Isthmus in 1941. The *Jääkärit* were eventually split between the *Panssaridivisioona* (JP 2 to JP 5) and the *Ratsuväkiprikaati* (JP 1 and JP 6). The frontier companies and battalions, spread from the northern shores of Lake Ladoga along the Finnish/Soviet border up to the Arctic, were amalgamated into eight Frontier battalions and redesignated as *Jääkärit* thanks to their impressive performance in the Winter War, while the five *Sissipataljoonaat* (Sissi battalions, *Sissi* translates as 'guerrilla'), made up of regular Finnish Army light-infantry troops that were lightly armed and equipped to facilitate Ranger-style operations, had dropped to two by 1941, each with a strength of around 1,000 men and a role much more akin to standard infantry than the guerrilla-style tactics that they were originally expected to employ.

RECRUITMENT, TRAINING AND MORALE

Soviet

On the eve of war the Red Army appeared to be fully recovered from its 1939–40 debacle in Finland, though there were significant problems that became apparent on closer inspection. The Red Army's system of recruitment, though far larger than any other peacetime army, was beset with shortcomings. Although the system of universal conscription had been the practice in the inter-war years and garnered around 1,500,000 men a year, one-third were disqualified for health or other reasons, and of the remainder there was only the facility to train 650,000 men, the

A pair of Soviet soldiers await an enemy attack in a foxhole. The hand grenades to the fore are a pair of F1 'Limonka' anti-personnel fragmentation hand grenades (derived from a French design that became popular during World War I – the 'Limonka' (lemon) nickname derived from their shape and yellow-green paint), and two RG-42 anti-personnel fragmentation hand grenades. The RG-42 was something of a stopgap weapon, a simpler version of the RGD-33 anti-personnel fragmentation stick grenade which was more labour-intensive to produce. Both types used the same 3.2–4.2-second UZRGM fuzes (Universalnyi Zapal, Ruchnaya Granata, Modernizirovannyi, 'Universal Igniter, Hand Grenade, Improved'), weighed more or less the same (the F1 was 600g, the RG-42 500g), and could be thrown about 35–40m; the main difference between the two was that the RG-42 had an effective blast radius of 10m while that of the F1 was 30m, making it necessary to throw the F1 from cover to avoid injury to the user. (From the fonds of the RGAKFD in Krasnogorsk via Stavka)

rest receiving only the barest introduction to military life (Dunn 2009: 45). For those who did receive training, their instruction left much to be desired, with little attention paid to small-unit tactics or larger manoeuvres, conscripts finding themselves more often used as casual labour or farmhands than as soldiers. On the eve of Operation *Barbarossa* the Soviet Union had expanded the Red Army to over 2,900,000 men, but the appalling damage done in the first six months of the Great Patriotic War (June 1941–May 1945), when 4,473,000 men were lost, strained the state's ability to maintain trained replacements.

In spite of the enormous losses ensuing from the German envelopments of cities such as Kiev and the almost immediate collapse of some formations as soon as they entered combat, other units stood firm, sometimes fighting beyond any hope of success or relief. The promotion of reliable units to Guards status in recognition of their efforts was one of the first successful practical steps that the Stavka took to bolster morale. Initial exhortations for the people to fight for the Communist Party were giving way by the end of 1941 to more traditionally patriotic mantras designed to appeal to the country's nationalist sentiment. The gradual stabilization of losses throughout 1942 and 1943 allowed the Red Army more breathing room, with divisions having the chance to rebuild rather than simply being fought to destruction. This in turn allowed cadres of experienced officers, NCOs and men to develop institutional knowledge that they could pass on to replacement drafts, resulting in fighting units becoming more effective.

Finnish

Upon reaching the age of 18 men were liable for conscription (350 days for enlisted men; 440 days for NCOs and officers), and were subject to recall at intervals for refresher training that was conducted at a number of regional centres based around the country. In the aftermath of the Winter War the Finnish government undertook several measures to bolster the nation's battered defences, including a doubling of the length of national service from one to two years. The majority of Finnish reserve units were raised in discrete local areas drawing on men who often knew one another in civilian life, with the resulting benefit that such units enjoyed a high level of comradeship. Independent battalions and other such units were mostly raised from the border areas where they were expected to operate. Civic education reinforced Finnish nationalism, something that was carried over into the regular education that conscripts received and which was often exemplified in the pages of the popular weekly magazine *Suomen Sotilas* ('Finland's Soldier') (Ahlbäck 2014: 110).

The Suojeluskunta (SK, 'Civil Guard') was distinct from the regular Army, though it too had its origin in the Finnish Civil War. Formed as a national civil-defence organization, it numbered 119,500 men in 1939, over half of whom would go on to serve in the Finnish Army during the Winter and Continuation wars. It offered sporting activities and, as time went on, more paramilitary-type training to Finnish youths, with an emphasis on shooting, physical fitness and skiing that left its members well-prepared for the rigours of Army life. From 1929 the Civil Guard established large-

Vuosalmi, 20 July 1944: a Finnish machine-gun crew lie ready at their 7.62×54mmR m/09-21 Maxim in a concealed firing position. The Maxims used by the Finns came from a number of sources, not least the large numbers captured from the Soviets during the Winter War (such guns being designated m/09-09 in Finnish service), and utilized either Sokolov wheeled mounts (with their defensive plate discarded) or purpose-built tripods, though the latter were primarily utilized by the domestically converted m/32–33 Maxims. (SA-kuva 156141)

scale military training and manoeuvres that focused not only on the use of small arms but also that of machine guns, mortars, artillery guns and signals equipment. General battlefield tactics and (to a lesser extent) military engineering techniques were taught as well as marksmanship, a process of education that proved useful in keeping skills fresh and ensuring that Army members and Reserve officers remained in a high state of training for longer periods, as well as promoting patriotism and a sense of duty (Jowett & Snodgrass 2006: 24).

Morale throughout the Finnish Army was generally high, sometimes exceptionally so. There had still been latent divisions within Finnish society left over from the Finnish Civil War, but these had paled into insignificance in the face of the massive Soviet onslaught of December 1939, an act that united the country as only an existential threat can. Though the Winter War ended in defeat the Finns could take some pride in how well they had fought against a vastly superior foe, and they could also nurse a justified sense of grievance over the annexation of the Karelian Isthmus and the forcible relocation of 12 per cent of the Finnish population that had resulted from it. Both factors served to stiffen Finnish resolve in the campaign of 1941 which was cast as an act of national recovery, though there were doubts about the decision to press on past recaptured Finnish territory into traditional Russian lands. The low-intensity period of trench warfare during 1942–44 also seemed to have some negative impact, with Finnish soldiers wondering why they were still at war when they already had their lands back.

TACTICS AND WEAPONS

Soviet

The Red Army of 1941 was in a state of transition, and had not yet fully come to terms with the damage inflicted on its officer corps (and the intellectual work that it produced) by the wave of Stalin's purges that had started in 1937. The majority of the Red Army's senior leadership down to divisional level had been imprisoned, exiled or executed, leaving callow subordinates promoted into roles for which they had little training and no experience. One result of such a loss of veteran leadership was a corrosive lack of trust among Soviet commanders in their superiors as well as their subordinates, exemplified by the ubiquity of political officers (Politruks) and commissars at every level of the Red Army. Operations were often planned with excessive rigour to ensure that all responsibilities and objectives were delineated in the greatest possible detail, with little or no appreciation of the benefits of individual initiative. There were also failings in the systems of command and control, exemplified by the overly administrative structure of the Red Army's rifle corps, the unwieldy nature of its rifle divisions, and the confusion over how best to employ armour on the battlefield – the bold penetrations envisaged by Marshal Mikhail Nikolayevich Tukhachevsky that would open up the enemy's heart to deep operations had seemingly died with him upon his execution on 12 June 1937, with a more timid role in support of attacking infantry being favoured in the more chilling atmosphere of 1941. The price for such problems would be counted in millions of dead Red Army personnel before the year was out.

Offensive strategies were initially rather simple, with the infantry expected to play the key role in forcing the breakthrough supported by tanks, artillery and aviation. The offensive capabilities of massed armour were underappreciated and the infantry, through a combination of indifferent training, equipment shortages and poor leadership, lacked tactical flexibility and initiative. In the defence such shortcomings, so glaring in the attack, became less important, and the oft-noted stubbornness of Soviet units in the battles around Lake Ladoga in 1941 would cause the Finns real problems in their attempt to retake Karelia.

By the time Stalin was ready to bring his focus back to Finland in the early summer of 1944, the Red Army had undergone a number of significant changes that made it a more formidable foe. Infantry tactics had changed, partly in acknowledgement of the fact that the supply of men was not inexhaustible, partly to take advantage of weapons such as the PPSh-41 and PPS-43 SMGs, and partly due to the application of combined-arms tactics – a form of warfare that demanded a level of skill and initiative on the part of the participating forces that was rarely present in the early months of the war, and for those same forces to have practised with one another in realistic exercises. The experience accrued by the Red Army over the preceding three years told in its favour, with many of the rifle divisions and Guards rifle divisions of 1944 enjoying a much better understanding of how to work with other arms, use terrain and employ initiative to their advantage.

Infantry, artillery, armour and aviation were expected to operate in support of one another; the first phase of an operation required in-depth planning to ensure the maximum concentration of forces at the enemy's most vulnerable point. In the second phase, air assets would saturate the area and destroy communication lines while the artillery bombarded prearranged targets; finally, every available artillery asset, centralized under one command, would concentrate a brief but extremely violent barrage immediately preceding the assault. The third phase was the assault itself with artillery provided for direct-fire support and – in a notable departure from the methods of 1941 – the movement of units and fire from supporting arms being subject to the initiative of local commanders. After the objective in the enemy's rear was reached, the attacking units would consolidate their positions, secure their flanks against counter-attacks, and prepare for the exploitation of the penetration (TM 30-430 1945: 21). Although such cooperation was often successful in the early stages of an operation, the deeper the attack penetrated the more likely it became that cohesion between the supporting arms would weaken, allowing the defenders to exploit the gaps that formed (Hill 2017: 485).

The basic doctrine of Soviet infantry was based on the rapid manoeuvring of small groups, the concentration of fire of automatic weapons, and shock action. In fluid situations, rapid deployment and immediate engagement with the enemy was the rule. In more stable situations an engagement with the enemy would be preceded by thorough reconnaissance and planning, as well as detailed rehearsal of the contemplated manoeuvre down to the actions of the individual soldier. Units would be deployed in line, wedge, inverted wedge or echelon formation, with the objective usually being a flank attack that resulted in a single or double envelopment. A regiment would normally attack across a front of 1,400m, a battalion 640m, a company 320m and a platoon 90m, in each case with a portion of the force held back as a reserve. Reconnaissance scouts would determine enemy positions, the SMG companies would often be employed as flanking forces or as part of the reserve, the mortars would be used in support of the initial attack as well as for any defensive bombardments, while other artillery assets and anti-tank guns were used in the direct-fire role to support the assault.

Tanks, though still not as vaunted as they had been in Tukhachevsky's visions of the 1930s, had a much more central part to play in the penetration of enemy defences. Tank attacks were usually conducted in a deeply echeloned formation on a narrow sector, using their fire and shock power to achieve penetration. Resistance was bypassed in order to avoid full deployment and protracted local combat, with accompanying infantry and artillery detailed to mop up enemy strongpoints and provide flank security for the armoured force against enemy counter-attack. Tank riders were a common feature of any tank assault, the accompanying infantry alighting from the vehicle when combat was imminent, allowing them to move forward and engage enemy infantry or anti-tank defences. Medium tanks such as the T-34 and T-34-85 were the backbone of tank attacks, while heavy tanks such as the KV-1 and IS-2 were used en masse in the direction of the main effort, and always in coordination with medium tanks which protected their flanks and rear. The T-34s forced the commitment of enemy anti-tank weapons, which were then destroyed by heavy-tank fire. In operations against armour, particularly medium tanks, the heavy tanks attacked frontally, while the accompanying medium tanks enveloped the enemy flanks and rear. Only in the support of assault groups destroying emplacements were heavy tanks used in small separate detachments of two or three tanks. Infantry support for heavy tanks was imperative. Both heavy- and medium-tank formations would use self-propelled artillery to provide security by protecting their flanks and rear against armoured counter-attacks, usually operating from hull defilade or concealed positions, covering probable avenues of enemy tank approach (TM 30-430 1945: 76).

Finnish

The Finns had proved that they knew how to fight in the depths of winter, especially against an overweening and arrogant foe. The campaigns of 1941 and 1944, however, fought in the warm summer months, deprived the Finns of some of the natural advantages they had exploited so effectively in 1939–40, though their tactics remained largely unchanged. The use of *motti* tactics – the encirclement, division and systematic elimination of an enemy force – that had delivered such dramatic victories such as that seen at the Raate Road in early January 1940 were still attempted, notably at the battles around Ilomantsi in July–August 1944, though with less success, due to a combination of too few Finnish troops and more effective Soviet defences. There was an understanding that the Finnish Army should not rest on its laurels, with several books examining the recent campaigns such as Colonel Martti Vihma's 1942 study *sotakokemusten analysointi sekä ohjesääntöjen* ('Analysis of War Experience') and Lieutenant-General Hugo Österman's 1943 work *taktisten ohjesääntöjen uusiminen* ('Revision of Tactical Rules') being published, but there was no systemic approach to changing what, in most people's eyes, already appeared to be working. At the battalion or regimental level Finnish tactics were consistently effective, but there were definite shortcomings in the operation of larger forces – something that had not much featured in the more modestly sized pre-war training regime.

Squad tactics were based around the Lahti-Saloranta m/26 LMG and the Suomi KP/-31 SMG. The KP/-31 was very heavy but it was also accurate and highly effective in the hands of an experienced user, but the m/26, despite being home-grown, was often less popular than captured Soviet DPs (the m/26 was accurate but hard to maintain, and the 20-round magazines were considered too small in comparison to the DP's 47-round pan magazine). Finnish riflemen were usually good shots as a result of the Army's pride in marksmanship and the training provided by the Civil Guard, aspects that were reinforced by the high level of private rifle ownership and the practice of hunting that was extremely widespread in nearly all of Finland's rural areas. Medium machine guns available were usually Finnish 7.62×54mmR m/32–33 Maxims or captured Soviet 7.62×54mmR PM M1910 Maxims (often adapted to Finnish use). Close artillery support for infantry operations was primarily conducted by mortars; there were 13 different types of mortar in use at the start of the Continuation War, one of the most common calibres being 81mm with types including the Finnish-made 81 Krh/38 (up to 30rd/min with a maximum range of 2,850m); these were supplemented by many captured Soviet 82mm 82-PM-36 and 82-BM-37 examples (25–30rd/min with a maximum range of 3,040m), while the Finnish-made 120mm Krh/40 (up to 20rd/min with a maximum range of 5,300m) provided heavier support. More advanced combined-arms tactics were somewhat hampered by the relative paucity of artillery, armour and air power, with the exception of the *Jääkärit* and *Panssarijääkäripataljoonaat* of the *Panssaridivisioona*.

Defensive tactics were often designed around Finland's natural terrain, with features such as lakes, swamps, forests and rough ground providing excellent sites on which to establish machine-gun or artillery strongpoints with interlocking fields of fire in depth. Defending against tanks had been one of the more difficult challenges for the Finns during the Winter War, so the prospect of any future engagement with Soviet armour necessitated good anti-tank defences. The 20×138mmB Lahti L-39 anti-tank rifle had just missed the Winter War and would prove too light to engage the likes of the T-34 medium tank seriously, though its great accuracy and powerful cartridge made it effective against soft-skinned vehicles. There were a number of weapons in the

A soldier examines his Panzerfaust 30 single-shot anti-tank weapon in the Finnish defensive positions at Vuosalmi, 17 July 1944. Known in Finnish Army service as the *Panssarinyrkki* ('armour fist') F2, an improvement on the earlier model *Faustpatrone klein*, known as the *Panssarinyrkki* F1, it weighed 5.2kg (2.9kg of which was the shaped-charge warhead), was 104.5cm long, and could penetrate 200mm of armour at a range of up to 30m. The very similar looking Panzerfaust 60, which used the same warhead but employed a more powerful launch tube to double the weapon's effective range, would not appear on the Finnish front in any numbers. (SA-kuva 156046)

25–37mm range, but captured Soviet 45mm M1932 and M1937 anti-tank guns were more useful. Ten Austrian 4.7cm Böhler 32 and 12 Italian 47mm Cannone da 47/32 mod. 35 anti-tank guns had been bought from Switzerland and Italy respectively after the Winter War, serving as the 47 PstK/35 and 47 PstK/39, but the results were mixed, unlike the 50mm 50 PstK/38 anti-tank gun (the Finnish designation for the 5cm German PaK 38) which proved popular and effective, 27 being ordered in August 1942. The 50 PstK/38 could knock out the T-34, though it was heavy and difficult to transport in comparison with the smaller-calibre anti-tank guns, all of which could be manhandled by their crews.

The heaviest anti-tank guns were both 75mm – the 75 PstK/97-38 and the 75 K/40 (the Finnish designation for the German 7.5cm PaK 40). The Finns bought 46 of the 75 PstK/97-38 (a combination of two guns: the barrel of the French M1897 75mm gun and the carriage of the German PaK 38), and it proved to be effective enough but with a severe recoil that made it unpleasant to operate. The 75 K/40 was a first-class 'tank killer' and would prove to be the backbone of the Finnish Army's anti-tank gun companies in 1944; a total of 130 were available by 20 March 1944, with further deliveries of 40 more guns in July and a final 40 in August.

The arrival of the Panzerfaust 30 single-shot anti-tank weapon in the spring of 1944 brought with it great tank-killing potential, but relatively few Finns had been taught how to use the *Panssarinyrkki* ('armour fist') F2 by the time the hammer fell – of the 25,000 available only 4,000 were used in combat (Jowett & Snodgrass 2006: 56). More traditional methods of tank killing in the form of Molotov cocktails and satchel charges were still employed. The newer Soviet tank designs were much less susceptible to the original cocktail's incendiary properties, however, and as a result it had been retired in 1942, replaced by the *sokaisupullo* ('blinding bottle') m/44, essentially a powerful smoke bomb that would blind the Soviet tank's crew, allowing Finnish infantry to close with the vehicle and destroy it. The satchel charge was actually two types of weapon: the first was a Finnish version of the German *Geballte Ladung* ('bundled charge'), an m/32 *varsikranaatti* ('stick grenade') with half-a-dozen extra heads wired around the main charge, that was known in Finnish service as a *hyökkäsvaunukäsikranaatti* ('anti-tank hand grenade'); the second was a series of factory-made charges known as 'Kasapanos': 2kg, 3kg or 4kg rectangular blocks of TNT in a sheet-metal box attached to the handle of a stick grenade. A range of anti-tank mines (the Panssarimiina m/36, m/39, s/39, s/40 and m/44) were also developed, such weapons often proving effective in the close and difficult terrain of Karelia.

A Soviet bunker is destroyed by a Finnish engineer using an m/40 flamethrower, 2 November 1941. The *liekinheitin* ('flamethrower') m/40 was the Finnish designation for the Italian Lanciaflamme Spalleggiabile Modello 35, 176 of which had been purchased during the Winter War, though most arrived too late to see any service. Weighing 25.5kg, the m/40 could fire 20–30 one-second bursts of flame out to a maximum range of 20m, and used a different fuel mix depending on the season (the summer mix was two-thirds heavy fuel oil to light oil; the winter mix added gasoline). Initially organized into six-flamethrower platoons attached to engineer battalions, by September 1943 they had been reorganized into the *Jääkaripioneeri joukkue* (*Jäger* Engineer Battalion) that had 12 flamethrowers operating in six two-man teams. (Keystone-France/Gamma-Keystone via Getty Images)

COMMUNICATIONS

Soviet

Soviet troops, most likely *Razvedchiki* ('scouts'), pause to use their radio. Their being *Razvedchiki* is probable because of the way they are armed (with PPSh-41 SMGs) as well as their 'amoeba'-pattern camouflage smocks, which were usually only issued to specialist units such as scouts, snipers, engineers and airborne troops. The radio is an RBM (RBM, RB-M: *Radiostantsiya Batalonnaya Modernizirovannaya*, 'Modernized Battalion Radio'), one of the most common sets produced during the war from 1942 onwards; it weighed 13kg and operated within the frequency range 1.5–5MHz, a small whip antenna giving it a range of 10km for voice communication and 15km for telegraphy (a mast antenna could increase these ranges to 30km for voice and 50km for telegraphy). (Courtesy of the Central Museum of the Armed Forces, Moscow via Stavka)

In 1941 a Red Army rifle regiment's signal company was equipped with a 5-AK radio (entering service in 1929, the 5-AK was operated by a team of 3–5 men and usually mounted on a vehicle or two-wheeled cart), a pair of 6-PK radios, two wire/optical platoons, a messenger section and a switchboard team. The 6-PK operated in the frequency range 3.75–5.25MHz and had a range of 3–8km for telephone and 6–15km for telegraph communications. On paper a rifle battalion's signal platoon had three wire/optical squads and three telephone carts (22 men in total), as well as a seven-man radio group equipped with four backpack RRU transceivers and a 6-PK radio; wiremen were attached to the machine-gun company HQ and mortar company HQ, while each rifle company HQ and platoon HQ had a runner (Zaloga & Ness 2009: 7). In reality, the long-running inefficiencies in supply and training coupled with battlefield losses meant that, below regimental level, the runner was the most common method of communication. Armoured elements were slightly better favoured with radio equipment (though the importance of tank-to-tank communication was woefully underappreciated – for example, in the T-26 and BT-7 light tanks radios were only usually installed in command vehicles, with flares, flags and hand signals used to communicate between most vehicles), but reconnaissance, anti-tank and anti-aircraft units had no dedicated radio sets at all. By 1943 the lack of radios in tanks was largely remedied, most T-34s having a 9R or 9RM AM transceiver (the latter having a range of 9km), while the T-34-85 used an improved version, the 9RS, introduced during 1944.

The situation for rifle divisions had also improved somewhat by 1944, though mainly through the auspices of Lend-Lease which accounted for 88 per cent of Soviet communications equipment, with up to 380,000 field telephones and 245,000 radios supplied by the US (including large numbers of SCR-300, -511, -536 and -584 sets), and many other radios, along with EE-8 field telephones and 1.6 million kilometres of telephone wire to augment the often poorly made Soviet version (Rottman 2010: 32–33). The UNA-F-28 and UNA-F-31 were, along with the American EE-8, the most common portable front-line field telephones, while transceivers like the A-7 (from November 1942) and the A-7A (from May 1943) – operating within the frequency range 27–32Mhz – provided rifle and artillery regiments with a reasonable radio, when they were available. The A-7 sets had a range of 3–4km in urban environments, 7–8km in rough country and up to 10km in the open; the set weighed 15.5kg, with the batteries weighing 6kg and giving 35–40 hours of continuous use on a full charge.

Finnish

In the wake of the Winter War the Finns were still suffering from a shortage of arms and equipment in many areas, including communications – a situation exacerbated by the Soviet Union's belligerence towards any country that could prove a useful trading partner to Finland. Nevertheless, some much-needed radio equipment did arrive from France, Sweden and Hungary in mid-1940 that augmented the existing Finnish home-grown systems. The Finns classified their field-radio requirements as follows: corps-level (AB-), divisional-level (B-), sub-unit level (C-) and artillery (D-). The main battalion-level set was the C-Radio VRFK which operated within the frequency range 3.0–6.0MHz, while the main artillery sets employed were evolutions from a 1927 design, the P12-15 (VRGK 9/1941) and P12-15A (VRGKA 1942). Radios were rarely available below battalion level, which had an impact on the ability of local commanders to call up timely artillery support or reinforcements when in the attack, though a good telephone network

A Finnish radio operator using an unidentified radio set (possibly a captured older Soviet model) near the front line at Syskyjärvi, 30 August 1944. As with many other areas of weaponry and equipment, the Finns were short of every type of radio, with preference being given to the artillery. Many Soviet radio sets of various designs were captured during the Winter War, and were pressed into Finnish service along with small numbers of domestic radio sets as well as those purchased internationally. (SA-kuva 162336)

supplemented by well-plotted target grids ensured that timely artillery fire was usually available for defensive positions. In the event of field-telephone communications failing a system of signal flares could be used to draw fire down on prearranged spots.

There were also 165 radio sets captured from Soviet rifle and armoured units during the Winter War that were employed against their former owners, a number that would increase substantially thanks to the spoils of the 1941 campaign. After the alliance with Germany various German radio sets also found their way into Finnish service, such as the Funkgerät 5 and Funkgerät 8 that were used in the StuG IIIs assigned to the *Panssaridivisioona*.

The Finns also developed an effective radio set for their long-range reconnaissance patrols – the M10 Kyynel High Frequency transceiver. The Kyynel ('Tear') was first designed under the auspices of the lead engineer Captain Holger Jalander, fielded as a receiver (the M4) in 1941, issued with a transmitter (the M7) towards the end of that year before evolving into the M10 transceiver by early 1942. It operated within the frequency range 3.3–4.8MHz with a power output up to 0.5W and a range varying from 64km to over 600km, due to the fact that the Kyynel was a high-frequency radio: its communication range was a function of both the exact frequency being used as well and the time of day or night that transmission was taking place. Measuring 5.5×12×24cm and weighing only 1.6kg, the M10 Kyynel was fully enclosed in an aluminium case and carried in a reinforced-cardboard container with a carrying strap – perfect for long-distance operations.

A veteran of the Winter War and the Siege of Leningrad, General Kirill Afanasievich Meretskov would lead the Vyborg–Petrozavodsk Offensive in June 1944 followed by the Petsamo–Kirkenes Offensive on 7 October, the success of which would see him promoted on 26 October to the rank of Marshal. (Sovfoto/Universal Images Group via Getty Images)

Field Marshal Carl Gustaf Emil Mannerheim was the man responsible for Finland's epic defence in the Winter War, as well as the 1941 campaign to reconquer those Finnish lands lost to the Soviet Union. On 4 August 1944 the Parliament of Finland conferred the nation's presidency upon him, thus uniting the nation's political and military leadership in one man. Through his undoubted military ability and leadership Mannerheim helped ensure that Finland emerged from the war as an independent state. (© CORBIS/Corbis via Getty Images)

LEADERSHIP

Soviet

The Red Army experienced failings of leadership at every level during the Winter War. The subsequent changes initiated within the Army had not taken root before the invasion of 22 June 1941, a situation exacerbated by the Army's rapid expansion. The system of dual command – whereby an officer had a political equal to ensure his loyalty as well as countersign any orders he might issue – was an obvious hindrance, but by late 1941 command became more streamlined as the political officers were removed from direct involvement in military operations.

While those who had attended technical schools for aviation or engineering were destined for well-regarded military roles, junior infantry officers were generally undertrained and any further education was the purview of an officer's regiment and division. As these junior officers were responsible for training the men under their command, the gaps in their knowledge coupled with their own lack of experience meant that they were often unable to impart even the most basic lessons of doctrine and tactics to their charges (Reese 1996: 164). This situation was compounded by the absence of a professional NCO corps within the Army. By November 1940 the ranks of *Stárshiy Serzhánt* ('Senior Sergeant'), *Serzhánt* ('Sergeant') and *Mládshiy Serzhánt* ('Junior Sergeant') had been reinstated. By 1944 there were enough men with enough experience to provide their units with effective non-commissioned officers; even so, the distribution of talent was uneven.

Finnish

Within the Finnish Army there was a great deal of respect for the more senior officers, many having served in World War I, the Finnish Civil War and the Winter War. There was a unifying patriotism that helped bond men to their officers, but such loyalty was not a given, especially in the distinction between reserve troops and the regulars. Knut Pipping, who served in Jalkaväkirykmentti 12 (Infantry Regiment 12) during the Continuation War, noted that the majority of NCOs and junior officers were reservists, with only company commanders and some of the older NCOs being regulars.

These professionals were seen as being keener on discipline and less sensible in organizing work. Reserve officers were also treated with occasional superciliousness by their regular compatriots (Pipping 2008: 127).

Despite the sense of common cause that could develop between reservist men and reservist officers, there was still a notable distinction between the two groups, mainly determined by the level of education the officers had attained in civilian life, as well as the belief that in the end they were on the same side as the regular officers where the war was concerned. As with most armies, the young officers that shared the hardships of their men, slept in the same grim billets and undertook the same risks as they did, would often be exempted from the more general disparagement directed at their class.

Sortavala

10 July–15 August 1941

BACKGROUND TO BATTLE

With the launch of Operation *Barbarossa* on 22 June and the subsequent Soviet aerial bombing raids against Finnish airfields, major cities and industrial centres on 25 June, war was a reality once again. Mannerheim, with his plans for the re-conquest of lost Finnish lands, shifted the Finnish Army from a defensive to an offensive posture, though the situation he faced was very different from that of December 1939. The Army was in a much better state of preparedness, with considerably more artillery guns (and crucially the ammunition with which to feed them) than in the Winter War, even if there were still shortages of communications equipment and a negligible armoured capability. Another important element was Finland's alliance with Germany, which provided a measure of security in matters of supply as well as security on Finland's Baltic and Arctic flanks.

The most significant factor, however, was the German invasion of the Soviet Union, prosecuted with unimaginable intensity over those first few weeks and resulting in catastrophic losses for the Red Army and the VVS (Voyenno-Vozdushnye Sily, 'Military Air Forces'). In the first few weeks of the new war the Finns did not launch any major offensives in concert with their notional German allies, giving the Stavka enough peace of mind to treat the Karelian theatre as of secondary importance. As a direct result, Red Army units protecting the Soviet–Finnish border were sent south to help try to stem the relentless advance of the German war machine, leaving Soviet defences north of Leningrad weakened and unlikely to receive reinforcements any time soon. As a result the Finnish forces found themselves in the unusual position of enjoying local dominance, the historian Olli Vehviläinen noting how during the campaign by Lake

Soviet soldiers from an SMG squad on the attack. The Red Army had learned its lesson concerning the effectiveness of the SMG in the Winter War, but the PPD-40 – the Soviet Union's existing SMG – was difficult to manufacture in anything like the required quantities. The PPSh-41 was the answer, being fielded in small numbers towards the end of 1941 and in significantly more substantial numbers thereafter. The value of the PPSh-41 was recognized in the increase of the number of submachine-gunners in an infantry squad from one to two, as well as the formation of entire SMG companies by the middle of the war. (Nik Cornish at www.stavka.org.uk)

Ladoga the Finns had a four-to-one superiority in infantry and a nine-to-one superiority in artillery (Vehviläinen 2002: 93).

The Stavka's confidence in Finnish passivity was misplaced. There would not likely be a better chance for the Finns to regain what they had so recently lost, but when it came the main Finnish effort would not be a direct assault on the most obvious objective of Viipuri and the rest of the Karelian Isthmus, but rather against Soviet forces positioned to the north of Lake Ladoga. Mannerheim's supposition was that Karelia would be much more heavily defended, and that it might prove prudent to keep a degree of distance between initial Finnish operations and those conducted by the Germans – there was little desire among the Finns to be seen as acting in direct support of Generalfeldmarschall Wilhelm Ritter von Leeb's Heeresgruppe Nord (Army Group North) in its march on Leningrad (Johansen 2016: 183). Mannerheim's objective was the city of Sortavala on the northern bank of Lake Ladoga, driving straight for the junction between the Soviet 7th and 23rd armies. Once Sortavala had been taken, Soviet forces north and south of Lake Ladoga would be cut off from one another, and the campaign to retake Karelia would begin.

The main Finnish forces consisted of IV Corps and II Corps on the Karelian Isthmus, and the Army of Karelia, established by Mannerheim on 29 June, commanded by Lieutenant-General Erik Heinrichs (Mannerheim's chief of staff) and which consisted of VII Corps (Major-General Woldemar Hägglund), VI Corps (*Jäger* Major-General Paavo Talvela) and Group Oinonen (Major-General Woldemar Oinonen), arrayed to the north of Lake Ladoga. VII Corps consisted of 7. and 9. divisions; VI Corps consisted of 5. and 11. divisions, 1. Reserve Division and 1. JPr (*Jääkäriprikaati*, 'Jäger Brigade'); Group Oinonen consisted of 2. JPr, the RvPr (*Ratsuväkiprikaati*, 'Cavalry Brigade') and Sissipataljoona 1 (Sissi Battalion 1). Both IV Corps and II Corps would maintain the line on the Karelian Isthmus, but II Corps, abutting the Army of Karelia's right (southern) flank, was prepared to move in support of VII Corps if need be.

Opposing the Finns were three Soviet armies consisting of 13 infantry divisions and one armoured division. The main Soviet forces included the

23rd Army (Lieutenant-General Pyotr Stepanovich Pshennikov) defending the Karelian Isthmus up to Sortavala on Lake Ladoga's northern bank, the 7th Army (Lieutenant-General Philip Danilovich Gorelenko) from the northern shore of Lake Ladoga up to the area east of Suomussalmi, with the 14th Army (Lieutenant Valerian Alexandrovich Frolov) responsible for the remainder of the border up to the Barents Sea.

Despite the accounts of relative calm on the Finnish–Soviet front during the initial days of Operation *Barbarossa*, Major Andrei Matveyevich Andreyev, commander of the 5th Border Detachment of the NKVD (Naródnyiy Komissariát Vnútrennikh Del, 'People's Commissariat for Internal Affairs'), claimed that at 0500hrs on 22 June Finnish artillery fire began raining down on Red Army fortifications and NKVD border outposts, particularly near the northern outskirts of the city of Enso. The following days saw a number of small-scale Finnish scouting parties attempt to penetrate all along the border, something the Soviets were certainly undertaking as well.

The situation escalated dramatically on the morning of 29 June, with the conflict at Enso being typical of the type of engagements occurring all along the Karelian and Ladoga fronts, two Finnish infantry battalions supported by tanks seizing the town after a three-hour struggle. A Soviet counter-attack was quickly pulled together, the report of the action describing how with the rapid response of the NKVD border guards under the command of the chief of the outpost, Senior Lieutenant Bebyakin (who was wounded in the battle), the Soviet forces drove the Finns out of Enso and inflicted on them a number of casualties in the process, as well as forcing them to leave behind two wrecked tanks, a pair of machine guns and 70 magazines of ammunition (quoted in Andreyev 1984: 21). However gallant the defence put up by the NKVD border guards, it could not withstand the attack of two Finnish reinforced infantry divisions on the night of 1/2 July that pushed the defenders back in attacks that were replicated all along the front. Even so, the main Finnish offensive was yet to begin.

An infantry detachment of the Finnish Army marching towards the front lines, Karelia, June 1941. This is likely an active Army unit rather than a reserve formation judging by the high number of helmets worn by the soldiers (unsurprisingly, the best and most modern equipment was sent where it was most likely to be needed). Note the soldier in the centre armed with what appears to be a 7.62×53mmR m/27 bolt-action rifle and a *varsikranaatti* ('stick grenade') m/32. His German M1911-style triple-cell ammunition pouches are not attached to the belt but are tied on with string – a common enough practice among SMG gunners for KP/-31 drum magazines, but somewhat idiosyncratic for a rifleman. (Mondadori via Getty Images)

MAP KEY

1 **10 July:** The Army of Karelia crosses the border, VII Corps attacking to the west of Lake Jänisjärvi and VI Corps to its east, with Group Oinonen protecting VI Corps' left flank.

2 **14 July:** 1. JPr and 5. Division capture Loimola, destabilizing the Soviet right (northern) flank. By 16 July elements of the force have reached Koirinoja on the shores of Lake Ladoga, cutting the Soviet forces in two.

3 **14–15 July:** The 260th Rifle Regiment is forced back by advancing Finnish forces, losing its commander and several other senior officers in the process.

4 **15–16 July:** VI Corps' 11. Division pushes the 367th Rifle Regiment and the 3rd Battalion of the 260th Rifle Regiment south along the eastern shore of Lake Jänisjärvi, and advances towards Hämekoski, Harlu and Läskelä.

5 **17–19 July:** The 402nd Rifle Division is threatened with encirclement and pulls back to a new defensive line. Repeated Finnish attacks finally result in troops of VII Corps joining up with infantry from VI Corps at the Jänisjoki River.

6 **29 July:** The 168th Rifle Division and the 198th Motorized Rifle Division launch a counter-attack to try to break through the Finnish advance, but the Soviet force lacks sufficient armour and artillery support and is repulsed.

7 **5–15 August:** Repeated Finnish attacks by 7. Division and 19. Division (in concert with 2. Division from 7 August) erode the Soviet positions around Sortavala. The Finnish flag is raised over the city on 15 August at 1510hrs, all Soviet troops having been driven out.

Battlefield environment

The environment around Lake Jänisjärvi and Lake Ladoga was hardly ideal territory for military operations, much of it being heavily forested and dotted with lakes, swamps, rivers and streams. Low hills, rocky outcrops and heights of granite were not uncommon, but there were also open areas cleared for farming, and numerous small villages and hamlets, sometimes of only a few buildings, were scattered throughout. Most roads were unmetalled, wearing quickly under heavy vehicles and raising plenty of dust when troops marched or carts rolled along them during the dry summer months. Although such constraints could work in favour of the defenders, most of their planned concrete defences were incomplete – the majority of field works were trench lines anchored by strongpoints at Jaakkima, Kangaskylä and Kumur made from earth and timber, supported by artillery batteries some kilometres behind the front. The main line of resistance had been established more or less along the border, with secondary positions further back. There was a railway line running south from Joensuu in Finland, crossing the border just to the west of Värtsilä and passing through Matkaselkä on its way to Sortavala. The railway line branched at Matkaselkä, running along the southern shore of Lake Jänisjärvi and heading east to Loimola. Sortavala itself lay at the head of one of the northern tributaries of Lake Ladoga.

An unfinished Soviet bunker at Kangaskylä, photographed during the Finnish advance towards Sortavala on 22 July 1941. Such fortifications (103 were built in support of the line held by the 168th and 71st Rifle divisions in the months before the attack) were a common feature of the Soviet defensive positions established throughout Karelia in the aftermath of the Winter War. As with this example they could be found in various states of completion and could be built from timber-reinforced earth, logs or concrete. Many were supplemented with other field fortifications including 27,496m of wire works (some electrified) and mines, though there was a shortage of the anti-personnel variety with artillery rounds sometimes being adapted as improvised explosive devices instead. Old Finnish fortifications usually faced eastwards and thus were of little use to the Soviets, with many of them dynamited by the Red Army after the Finnish Army's surrender in 1940. (SA-kuva 27911)

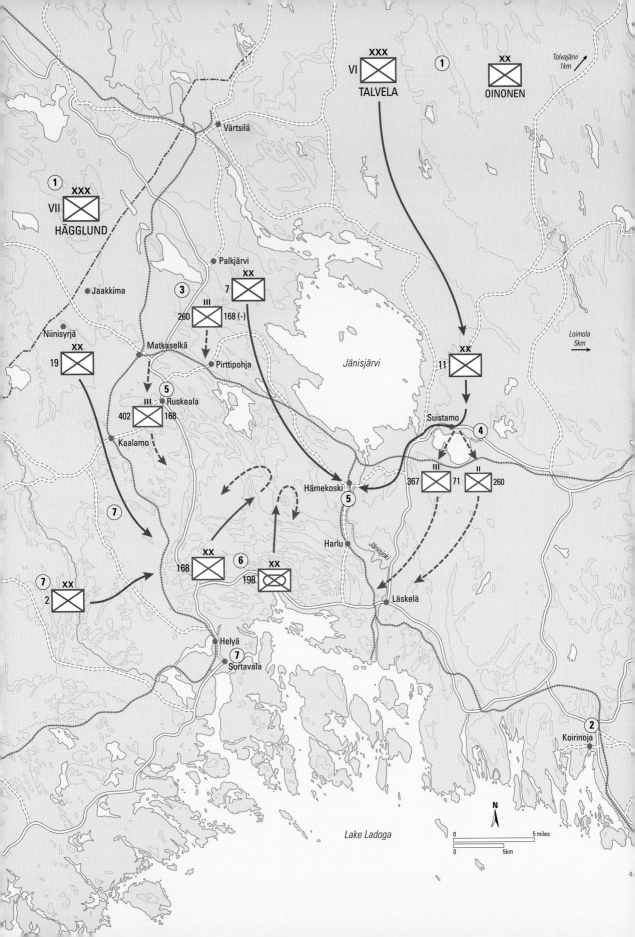

INTO COMBAT

In the early days of July, even though the formal instruction to launch the offensive had still to be issued, Finnish units engaged in serious attacks around Lake Jänisjärvi, probing Soviet defences and in some cases capturing their forward positions. On the evening of 9 July the order to move finally arrived at Heinrichs' headquarters and on the following day the Army of Karelia struck south, Hägglund's VII Corps advancing to the west of Lake Jänisjärvi heading directly for Sortavala, while Talvela's VI Corps advanced to its east towards Loimola, with Group Oinonen's cavalry and *Jäger* brigades protecting Talvela's left flank. The main thrust of VII Corps was led by Colonel Antero Svensson's 7. Division consisting of three infantry regiments (9, 30 and 51), the light detachment KevOs 15 (Kevyt Osasto 15, 'Light Detachment 15'), and KTR 2 (Kenttätykistörykmentti 2, 'Field Artillery Regiment 2'). Colonel Hannu Hannuksela's 19. Division (JR 16, JR 37, JR 58, KTR 10, KevOs 18) advanced on 7. Division's right (southern) flank. The relative lack of motorized transport in the Finnish forces was not much of a hindrance in terrain that was largely unsuitable for mechanized warfare, but their infantry (particularly the excellent *Jäger* of 1. and 2. JPr), made good progress, with the troops from Colonel Kaarlo Heiskanen's 11. Division capturing Värtsilä on 11 July. Such advances soon began to stall, however, when the Finns ran into the Soviets' main defensive line, a 62km-wide zone of fortifications manned by two of the 7th Army's rifle divisions – the 168th to the south-west and the 71st to the north-east – with Värtsilä at its centre.

Formed in Cherepovets in August–September 1939, the 168th Rifle Division, commanded since December 1939 by Colonel Andrei Leontyevich Bondarev (with Major Semyon Nikolaevich Borshchev as its head of operations), had endured the rigours of the Winter War, campaigning in the Sortavala region and remaining there as an occupying force after the war's end. Colonel Vasily Nikolaevich Fedorov's 71st Rifle Division, also of the 7th Army, was stationed to the 168th Rifle Division's right, while Major-General Semyon Petrovich Mikulsky's 142nd Rifle Division (23rd Army) was to the west. The 168th Rifle Division consisted of three rifle regiments (260th, 402nd, 462nd), the 453rd Field Artillery and 412th Howitzer Artillery regiments (226 pieces in all, including mortars), as well as anti-tank, anti-aircraft, reconnaissance, combat-engineer and communications elements. In the coming days the 168th Rifle Division would receive crucial support from the 367th Rifle Regiment, the 74th Separate Reconnaissance Battalion and the 237th Field Artillery Regiment (all from the 71st Rifle Division), as well as the 708th Rifle Regiment and other elements from the 115th Rifle Division.

The Soviet posture was defensive from the outset, with Gorelenko ordering the 71st and 168th Rifle divisions to man their prepared fortifications along the border, the 237th Rifle Division remaining in reserve to the east of Loimola. The defensive line of the 168th and 71st Rifle divisions was dominated by Lake Jänisjärvi, the 168th to the south-west of the lake and the 71st to the north-east of it. The supporting zone had been bolstered with a further 50km of trenches, anti-tank barriers,

4,500 anti-personnel and 3,000 anti-tank mines. The well-sited defensive network established by the two rifle divisions was enhanced in places with electrified-wire obstacles. On 7 July, Colonel N.T. Gritsay, commander of the 13th Separate Electrical Engineering Battalion, ordered one of his companies to set up a series of disguised electrified fences in support of existing positions, noting that one such entanglement established by Lieutenant I.Z. Chireikin's platoon near the Värtsilä border railway station would cause at least two-dozen casualties among the attacking Finns (Gritsay 1979: 185).

A more expansive account of the value yielded by such well-planned positions came from Lieutenant-Colonel A.M. Mitin, the second-in-command of the 402nd Rifle Regiment, who recalled how the defensive network on the approaches to Sortavala made the going much harder for the Finnish infantry, in this case likely to be men from Colonel Into Erkki Salmio's JR 37. Mitin noted how the effectiveness of the Soviet defence in these battles was achieved by the close interaction of fields of fire with engineering structures and barriers. A company of the 402nd Rifle Regiment under the command of Lieutenant Bekhtimirov, in cooperation with mortar support and sappers, fought for a day surrounded by two Finnish infantry battalions, winning the battle. Attacking a Soviet rifle company on the flank, one of the infantry battalions hit a disguised electrified fence; the Finns tried to tear through the metal mesh with grenades, and threw brushwood and the corpses of their dead soldiers onto it, but they were eventually pushed back under the fire of Lieutenant Zhuravlev's machine guns and the mortars of Junior Lieutenant Pavlov. Mitin thought that up to 300 Finnish corpses were left on the wire, and that this wasn't an isolated example of such an attack either (Mitin 1979: 178–79). Both of VII Corps' divisions as well as elements of VI Corps' 11. Division were initially held up by the Soviet line, the brunt of the initial defence falling upon the 402nd Rifle Regiment to the west and 367th Rifle Regiment to the east.

In VII Corps, 19. Division under Colonel Hannu Hannuksela was desperately understrength due to the majority of its troops being retained

Finnish infantry (wearing what are probably m/35 helmets) attack a Soviet bunker fortification that may well have been originally a converted Finnish position, sometime during the offensive in East Karelia, 1941. Most of the existing Finnish fortifications that had constituted the Mannerheim Line and other defences in Karelia had been systematically destroyed by the Soviets in the wake of the Winter War, though some remained and were adapted to the occupying forces' needs. Many others were still in the process of being constructed at the time of the Finnish attack in July 1941. (Ullstein bild/ullstein bild via Getty Images)

A nicely posed shot of a pair of Soviet soldiers operating their PTRD-41 anti-tank rifle. Weighing 17.4kg, the PTRD was a single-shot bolt-action weapon chambered for the 14.5×114mm armour-piercing round, the same ammunition utilized by the PTRS-41 semi-automatic anti-tank rifle. Although the PTRD-41's effective range was 300m, it was largely ineffective against German tanks unless used against the vehicles' sides or rear, and even then only at ranges under 100m. Despite such shortcomings the PTRD-41 was produced and issued in great numbers, and in Karelia it proved more of a threat against the mish-mash of older and more poorly armoured light tanks employed by the Finns. It was also useful as an anti-materiel weapon and could be employed against infantry strongpoints and even on occasion as an anti-aircraft weapon. (Courtesy of the Central Museum of the Armed Forces, Moscow via Stavka)

as part of the corps reserve. Hannuksela only had a single infantry regiment reinforced with an extra infantry battalion, but he hoped that a combination of surprise and weak Soviet forces would work to his advantage. Out of all the units of VII Corps, it was the attack by Hannuksela's 19. Division that jumped off furthest south and closest to the shores of Lake Ladoga; by avoiding main roads and manoeuvring through the forest, Hannuksela hoped to slip between two Soviet strongholds at Niinisyrjä and Repomäki and subsequently turn and take them in the rear. Unfortunately, his force was lacking in effective artillery support, but more significantly the resistance he encountered was far more substantial than he had expected. His division managed to advance little more than 5km during the first three days, after which a combination of extremely difficult terrain and the intensity of Soviet defences and counter-attacks saw all progress grind to a halt (Nenye 2016: 82). It was an experience shared to a greater or lesser degree by a number of other Finnish regiments in VII Corps and VI Corps.

On 14 July, after repeated attempts to drive a wedge into the Soviet line, the Finns overcame the resistance of the 2nd Battalion of the 260th Rifle Regiment and began to quickly move in the direction of Pirttipohja west of Lake Jänisjärvi. In an attempt to check the Finnish units that had broken through, the 187th Separate Reconnaissance Battalion and the 4th Company of the 462nd Rifle Regiment were urgently transferred from their existing defensive positions to plug the gap; with the support of artillery and mortar fire, they launched a decisive counter-attack that bloodied the Finnish advance and gave the Soviet line some breathing space. A Maxim machine-gun crew from the 187th Separate Reconnaissance Battalion commanded by Private Mikhail Dmitriev won fame during the encounter, repelling multiple Finnish infantry assaults that eventually forced the Finns to engage them with machine-gun fire and artillery. During the shelling the Maxim's machine-gunner Ukhanov was killed, but was quickly replaced by ammunition carrier Ilyin. Soon enough both Ilyin and the gun's observer, Divlekivdeyev, had been seriously wounded by shrapnel, forcing Dmitriev to fight on alone. A further shell strike finally disabled the machine gun and also broke Dmitriev's leg, but he continued to engage the enemy with a rifle until he ran out of ammunition, at which point he blew himself up with a hand grenade.

Despite such heroism the Finnish pressure was starting to tell. By 15 July to the east of Lake Jänisjärvi the 367th Rifle Regiment and the 3rd Battalion of the 260th Rifle Regiment were being driven southwards by regiments from Heiskanen's 11. Division, while 7. Division and 9. Division were pushing hard on the western side of the lake, albeit with less success than the troops of VI Corps. As a result of this sluggish advance, Hägglund decided to concentrate the forces of VII Corps against Matkaselkä in a renewed assault. Bondarev ordered Colonel V.F. Alekseev's 260th Rifle Regiment to stem the Finnish attacks, and a fierce series of battles developed around Ruskeala, Hämekoski and the Pirttipohja railway station, with the sites passing back and forth between the two sides on multiple occasions. With the Finns on the cusp of a breakthrough after the 260th Rifle Regiment's battalions finally broke, Alekseev organized and personally led his regimental reserve in a last-ditch counter-attack. It was a failure, with Alekseev, the regimental commissar, and the commander of the reconnaissance company (Major F.M. Oleinikov) all killed. Alekseev's replacement, Major P.F. Brygin, continued the fight.

Despite the relative success of the Soviet defence (mainly on the western side of Lake Jänisjärvi), to the north-east 1. JPr (Lieutenant-Colonel Väinö Merikallio) and 5. Division (Colonel Ruben Lagus) had broken through in an attack towards Tolvajärvi that resulted in the capture of Loimola on 14 July. That success behind the Soviet right (eastern) flank made

A Finnish crew man their Lahti L-39 semi-automatic anti-tank rifle amid burning houses on the Karelian Isthmus some 80km from Leningrad. Made by VKT (Valtion Kivääritehdas), the L-39 arrived too late to have much of an impact on the Winter War, and in the Continuation War its bulk (it weighed 49.5kg and was 220cm long) – not to mention its recoil – made it a difficult weapon to employ. It had a dual bipod with spiked legs for normal use and short skis for use on soft ground or in snow, the skis aiding transportation somewhat. It had a maximum range of up to 1,400m but the effective range would likely be less than half that. (T. Nousiainen/Hulton Archive/ Getty Images)

Surrounded at Kangaskylä, 16 July 1941

Junior Lieutenant I.I. Shishera's 2nd Battalion of Lieutenant-Colonel Ermakov's 402nd Rifle Regiment has been defending a line through the marshland and forests near the village of Kangaskylä, protecting the western (left) flank of the Matkaselkä–Sortavala road. On 13 July, Colonel Hannu Hannuksela's 19. Division smashed into the Soviet positions once again, attempting to overwhelm all three of the 402nd Rifle Regiment's understrength rifle battalions; for the past three days Shishera's men have repulsed numerous Finnish attacks, but on 16 July they discover that elements of Colonel Matti Laurila's JR 16 have outflanked them, putting the 2nd Battalion in danger of being surrounded. As Shishera attempts to pull

back to the south-east, the soldiers of one rifle platoon, led by Lieutenant Pyotr Budnik carrying a captured Suomi KP/-31 SMG, try to keep the Finns at bay with a ferocious counter-attack that soon devolves into a violent hand-to-hand struggle. Despite his inspirational leadership Budnik is cut down by a burst of automatic fire; his men, shaken and pressed by the attackers, cannot stop the Finnish noose from tightening. The 2nd Battalion, cut off from the rest of the 402nd Rifle Regiment and now fighting for its life, will manage to break out of the encirclement by nightfall, retreating through swamp-ridden forests for the next five days, eventually making it back to Soviet lines on 21 July.

the existing positions untenable, forcing the defenders to abandon their fortified line. Further problems arose for the Soviets from the continued predations of 1. JPr, which reached the Koirinoja crossroads on the shores of Lake Ladoga on 16 July, formally cutting off the 7th and 23rd armies from one another. At around the same time on the western side of Lake Jänisjärvi, the 402nd Rifle Regiment (Lieutenant-Colonel Ermakov) was having a particularly difficult time extracting itself from the line in the face of constant Finnish pressure and infiltrations, with its three rifle battalions subject to regular bouts of Finnish artillery fire as well as air attack from German aircraft as they tried to withdraw southwards. The 2nd Battalion (Junior Lieutenant I.I. Shishera) narrowly avoided being completely surrounded, and together with a battery of field artillery (which miraculously managed to retain all their guns) only just managed to fight clear of encirclement.

Heiskanen's 11. Division had pushed south along the eastern shore of Lake Jänisjärvi and by 21 July it had hooked around and began attacking towards the west, forcing the 367th Rifle Regiment back towards the precarious position of Bondarev's 168th Rifle Division. On the western side of Lake Jänisjärvi the Finns were driving forward in an attempt to cut the Matkaselkä–Sortavala road and make it to the Jänisjoki River, where they could link up with the approaching regiments of 11. Division. The initial push against the 402nd Rifle Regiment came on 17 July and broke through the Soviet line, requiring Bondarev to throw the 3rd Battalion of the 462nd Rifle Regiment and two companies of engineers into the breach to delay the Finnish advance. It was a temporary fix at best, with the Finns threatening to encircle the 402nd Rifle Regiment; but catching the Finns unawares, Bondarev pulled the rifle regiment back to a more defensible position during the night of 17/18 July, establishing the unit on a line that ran from Kaalamo to Ruskeala to the southern shore of Lake Jänisjärvi.

On the night of 18/19 July, another Finnish assault tried to break through the new line towards the southernmost point of Lake Jänisjärvi but ran straight into a counter-attack made up from a combined force of the 260th Rifle Regiment under Brygin and the 3rd Battalion of the 402nd Rifle

Members of a Soviet rifle squad sit around their DP LMG gunner during the earlier stages of the war. The DP, also called the DP-27 or DP-28 according to its year of adoption, used the same 7.62×54mmR cartridge as the Mosin-Nagant M91/30 bolt-action rifle and the PM M1910 Maxim medium machine gun, stored in a 47-round pan magazine that gave the weapon its nickname of *proigryvatel* ('record player'). It had a relatively low rate of fire, about 550rd/min, and was easy to control and operate, making it an effective light machine gun. Operated by a two-man team (the gunner and an assistant), its role within the 12-man rifle squad of June 1940 was to provide support for the attacking riflemen. By late 1942, however, a number of the new nine-man rifle squads were being issued with two DPs each – the bias had shifted from the rifle to the LMG, with the rifle squad's riflemen expected to replace casualties in the DP crews to ensure that the LMGs were always operable. Captured DPs proved equally popular with the Finns. (Courtesy of the Central Museum of the Armed Forces, Moscow via Stavka)

Regiment (Lieutenant Nikita Nazarovich Vorobyov), with the Soviets fighting the Finns to a standstill. The attackers did not let the matter lie, however, with many more attempts made, several of which ended in hand-to-hand combat, Vorobyov shouting for his men to engage with the bayonet. Despite such stout defence the Finns were too strong and the Soviets too thinly spread, and on 19 July Finnish units from VII Corps made it to the Jänisjoki River where they finally joined forces with troops from 11. Division in the area east of Hämekoski. The 367th Rifle Regiment, the 74th Separate Reconnaissance Battalion and the 230th Artillery Regiment of the 71st Rifle Division, all of which had been opposing 11. Division's advance, pulled back to the western bank of the river, joining forces with the battered regiments of the 168th Rifle Division. By 21 July the Soviet position was untenable, Bondarev pulling all his forces back towards Helyä in a fighting retreat and establishing a new defensive line there on 24–25 July.

To try to stabilize the situation, Major-General Vladimir Victorovich Kryukov's 198th Motorized Rifle Division was tasked with joining Bondarev's 168th Rifle Division in a counter-attack towards the Jänisjoki River. The 198th Motorized Rifle Division was initially stationed north-east of Viipuri but had moved into the areas around Elisenvaara by 2 July, where it was engaged in a number of actions and suffered heavy losses. Its organic tank regiment (the 146th) and both motorized rifle regiments (the 450th and 452nd) had been detailed elsewhere by the time it arrived in the vicinity of Sortavala, though it had acquired the 45th Tank Regiment as well as the 3rd People's Militia Regiment in recompense. The planned assault was hamstrung before it even began, however, thanks to the fact that the division's chief-of-staff – together with all the Soviet plans for the attack – was captured by the Finns on 28 July (Nenye 2016: 87). In the event the Soviet attack, launched at 0400hrs on 29 July and conducted by the 168th Rifle Division supported by tanks from the 198th Motorized Rifle Division, made some progress but lacked sufficient armour and artillery support to make much of a dent in the semicircle of encroaching Finns. By 1900hrs the advance had been halted by Finnish artillery and mortar fire, with a quickly deployed anti-tank screen wreaking havoc among the Soviet tanks. Its supporting armour destroyed, the 168th Rifle Division quickly retreated back to its starting positions. The 198th Motorized Rifle Division attempted another assault on 1 August but was easily repulsed once again, leading to its withdrawal from the line.

In the early days of August the already dire Soviet position became worse when Mannerheim, intent on cracking the nut of Sortavala, instructed Colonel Aarne Blick's 2. Division from II Corps to move north-east from its position on the Karelian Isthmus and join forces with 19. and 7. divisions in a final push to take the city. While Blick was on his way, on 5 August 19. Division and 7. Division broke through the centre and western flank of the Soviet line at multiple points, the penetrations including the use of small groups of submachine-gunners who infiltrated deep into the Soviet rear where they launched unexpected attacks, causing confusion and panic. By 6 August the 402nd, 260th and 462nd Rifle regiments had all been pulled back to yet another more defensible line, thereby tightening the noose around the Soviet forces as they did so.

With Blick's men arriving from the west the following day, the Finns launched another concerted attack, hemming Bondarev's regiments as well

A Finnish scout with a captured DP LMG takes up position overlooking Sortavala, 8 August 1941. Originally one of the most densely populated parts of Karelia, the city lay at the northernmost point of Lake Ladoga and had suffered from heavy bombing during the Winter War, its population subsequently evacuated to Finland as part of the Moscow Peace Treaty signed on 12 March 1940. (SA-kuva 34146)

as the 367th Rifle Regiment into an increasingly tight patch of land centred on Helyä and Sortavala, with only the waters of Lake Ladoga behind them. The 460th Rifle Regiment was in the best shape, but the 260th Rifle Regiment was down to two much-weakened battalions, and the rest of the Soviet units were not much better off. Significant amounts of weaponry had been lost but it was the shortage of communications equipment that was most concerning to Bondarev: it severely hampered his ability to exercise proper command and control over his fighting units, and also impacted on his ability to secure ammunition, food and other supplies from the rear echelons. From 11 August the Finnish attacks recommenced, slowly pushing Bondarev's men and those of the 367th Rifle Regiment deeper into the lands surrounding Sortavala, but despite this intense pressure the Soviet forces never broke and ran, instead maintaining their cohesion throughout their fighting retreat.

On 14 August all three Finnish divisions were organized into a new I Corps under Colonel Einar Mäkinen to streamline the command of the forces attacking Sortavala. In the event it hardly mattered as the final capture of the city came only a day later after another 24 hours of hard fighting, the Finnish flag being raised over the city's administrative building at 1510hrs on 15 August. Bondarev and the remains of his 168th Rifle Division withdrew from the city in good order and retreated down the coast towards Rautalahti Bay, where over 9,000 survivors commandeered a collection of barges and other watercraft and made their escape to the island of Valamo on Lake Ladoga.

To the east Talvela's VI Corps had forced its way southwards along the western bank of Lake Ladoga and into Karelia, while to the south-west IV Corps and the rest of II Corps were driving deep into the Karelian Isthmus. Efforts to recapture Karelia were meant to commence on 31 July on the assumption that Sortavala would have fallen by then, and even though that city remained in Soviet hands the advance towards Viipuri and Vuoksi began. Gradually the Soviet tactic of holding fast in the face of Finnish attacks no matter what gave way to fighting retreats, with Viipuri falling on 30 August and almost all the old Finnish lands secured by 2 September. Heeresgruppe Nord reached the southern shore of Lake Ladoga on 8 September, thus securing the Finnish victory and condemning Leningrad to the unanticipated horrors of an 872-day siege by German forces.

The Finns refused to offer further assistance in the investment or assaults on Leningrad, instead being content to launch one more operation to secure a buffer zone of Soviet territory in East Karelia. Mannerheim called a halt to further operations on 6 December after Medvezhyegorsk had fallen, the Finns then shifting to a defensive posture and concentrating on fortifying their newly won lands. To the south, however, the war was continuing with unabated ferocity, the German push on Moscow having stalled – indeed the first major Soviet counter-offensive in defence of their capital city had been launched on 5 December, a scant 24 hours before the Finns had ended their own advance. Mannerheim's expectation of a German victory over the Red Army, vital if he was to secure his country's recent gains, had yet to materialize.

A group of Finnish soldiers in m/36 summer uniforms gather around a captured gramophone at Jaakkima on 8 August 1941. The group give a good sense of how many Finnish Army units were armed and equipped, with two styles of cap and at least two types of helmet in view (Hungarian m/38s, distinguishable from the German m/35 by the flat metal loop on the rear of the neck guard, and Czech m/34s), as well as two men armed with captured SVT-40 gas-operated semi-automatic rifles. (SA-kuva 32422)

Kuuterselkä

14–15 June 1944

BACKGROUND TO BATTLE

A line of Soviet 122mm M1931/37 field guns firing on enemy positions. The M1931/37 was a corps-level or artillery-division asset that required a nine-man crew and was primarily used for indirect fire, though it could operate in the direct-fire role when engaging enemy armour. It could use armour-piercing or high-explosive shells (both types of projectiles weighing 25kg) out to maximum ranges of 4,000m and 19,800m respectively; in addition, there was a specialist anti-concrete shell for use against fortifications, also weighing 25kg and with a maximum range of 20,400m. The Finns captured 25 of these guns in the 1941 campaign (classed as the 122 K/31 in Finnish service), but due to a lack of suitable prime movers they were mostly relegated to coastal batteries. (Courtesy of the Central Museum of the Armed Forces, Moscow via Stavka)

The Finnish victories of 1941 brought no peace. The following years would see both sides settle into a stalemate of sorts, with localized incursions and relatively limited battles along the new border being the order of the day. There were Finnish successes, notably the capture of Suursaari Island and the exploits of their long-range reconnaissance patrols from Lake Ladoga up to the Arctic Circle, but Mannerheim's objective was stability, not further expansion. Despite ongoing Red Army operations against Karelia and other Finnish sectors, the main Soviet focus was on the sweeping offensives further south. That the tide of war on the Eastern Front had turned after the German defeat in the battle for Stalingrad (August 1942–February 1943) might have seemed clear enough to some, but the German Army, though on the defensive,

was far from a spent force, and there was no sense of when – or if – a Soviet victory in the Great Patriotic War might eventually come.

Friday 14 January 1944 saw the first stage of what the rest of the year promised, when the Red Army launched a major operation to break the siege of Leningrad once and for all, finally liberating that benighted city a month later. It was an important preparatory step before the long-gestating Operation *Bagration* – a momentous undertaking that aimed to destroy utterly the centre of the German line in Byelorussia – was to open that summer, but it did not necessarily herald another major assault on the Finns. There were obvious strategic benefits for the Soviets if Finland could be knocked out of the fight – exposing the German flank in the far north, the freeing-up of resources bogged down opposite Karelia, and the elimination of a real threat on the Soviet right during the anticipated summer offensive in Byelorussia – but political considerations also played their part; for Stalin it was better to have the Finns dealt with on his own terms, rather than as part of some post-war settlement (Lunde 2011: 271). The first Soviet attempt was diplomatic, with peace overtures in April 1944 on terms that were scarcely better than those of 1940, including a demand to restore the post-Winter War border, the demobilization of all Finnish forces and the equivalent of $600,000,000 in reparations (Lunde 2011: 260). In the face of a peace bought at the expense of much of its most valuable territory as well as any chance to defend itself in the future should the Soviets – now allied to the United States and Britain, the only significant powers the Finns could have looked to in order to help defend their interests – Finland rejected the Soviet offer. To be so summarily knocked back by the Finns was a rejection that proved both unexpected and infuriating to Stalin, and it initiated Soviet planning for a decisive attack on Finland.

The Red Army had formed two 'fronts' – the Leningrad Front directed against the Karelian Isthmus and the Karelian Front opposing East Karelia and the lands north of Lake Ladoga. The Leningrad Front consisted of the 21st Army (the western sector by the Gulf of Finland) and the 23rd Army (the eastern sector by Lake Ladoga); the 56th Army would also be attached from 29 June. The 23rd Army (Lieutenant-General Alexander Ivanovich Cherepanov) comprised the 98th Rifle Corps (177th, 281st and 372nd Rifle

An Ilyushin Il-2M 'Shturmovik' ('Storm Bird'), one of the most heavily produced ground-attack aircraft of World War II. It was well-armoured and carried a pair of fixed 23×152mm VYa-23 cannon and a pair of 7.62×54mmR ShKAS machine guns, all forward-firing, and one 12.7×108mm Berezin UBT machine gun mounted in the rear cockpit. It could carry rockets (either eight RS-82s or four RS-132s) to use against armour and strongpoints, or alternatively operate with a payload of either six 100kg bombs or 192 PTAB anti-armour bomblets. The 'Shturmovik' was heavily used in 1944's Vyborg Offensive, part of a concerted air campaign that helped break the Finnish lines at Valkeasaari and later Kuuterselkä. (Courtesy of the Central Museum of the Armed Forces, Moscow via Stavka)

A Red Army gun crew manhandle their 76mm M1942 artillery piece into position. The M1942 was a divisional field gun used both for indirect and (particularly) direct fire, the main projectiles being high-explosive rounds that each weighed 6.2–6.4kg and had a maximum range of 13,290m, though shrapnel, armour-piercing and HEAT rounds were also available. At only 1,116kg they were relatively easy guns to manoeuvre and had a high rate of fire, up to 25rd/min, making them highly effective in supplying close support to infantry and armour. The M1942 would also form the armament of the SU-76 self-propelled gun. (Courtesy of the Central Museum of the Armed Forces, Moscow via Stavka)

divisions) and the 115th Rifle Corps (10th, 92nd and 314th Rifle divisions). The 21st Army (Lieutenant-General Dmitry Nikolaevich Gusev, promoted to colonel-general on 18 June 1944) consisted of the 30th Guards Rifle Corps (Lieutenant-General Nikolai Pavlovich Simoniak, 45th, 63rd and 64th Guards Rifle divisions), the 97th Rifle Corps (Major-General Mikhail Mikhailovich Busarov, 178th, 358th and 381st Rifle divisions) and the 109th Rifle Corps (Lieutenant-General Ivan Prokopyevich Alferov, 72nd, 109th and 286th Rifle divisions). In addition, Gusev had 14 artillery, five tank and three assault-gun regiments in support of his rifle divisions. On the Karelian Isthmus against a 70km front (only 12–15km wide in the main operational zone of the western sector) the overpowering Soviet forces enjoyed a ratio of 4-to-1 in personnel, 5-to-1 in tanks, 6-to-1 in artillery and 15-to-1 in air power (Johansen 2016: 274).

The Red Army's plan (known as the Vyborg–Petrozavodsk Offensive) involved a two-stage strike; the first would be launched by the Leningrad Front against the Karelian Isthmus on 10 June, driving through the Valkeasaari crossroads towards the VT-Line, and from there on to Viipuri, taking the city by 20 June and going on to capture Helsinki by the middle of July. The second stage would be carried out by the Karelian Front against the Svir River line and Petrozavodsk on 21 June. There is some disagreement among the sources as to the ultimate limit of Soviet military–political objectives, but it seems reasonable to assume that, if the Red Army could not be stopped, Finland's fate would have been the same as that of the Baltic states in 1940 and again in late 1944.

The liberation of Leningrad in late January 1944 threw the possibility of a Soviet offensive against Karelia into sharp focus for the Finns, but their defences left much to be desired. The Main Line ran along the current border, and was bolstered by the VT-Line (from Vammelsuu on the Gulf of Finland to Taipale on the shores of Lake Ladoga), construction of which had begun in 1941. Unfortunately, despite the time available to the Finns the VT-Line was far from finished, and even those sections that had been completed were not as strong as they should have been, considering the size and strength of the enemy they would face. Two further defensive lines were initiated by Mannerheim on 18 November 1943, the VKT-Line (from Viipuri through Tali and Kuparsaari up along the northern bank of Vuoksi River and Suvanto to Taipale) and the U-Line north of Lake Ladoga. Despite the fact that an assault through the Karelian Isthmus was the overwhelmingly likely line of attack for the Red Army, completion of the defences was not attended to until far too late – something that was noticed by the Soviet intelligence services.

The Finnish units defending the Main Line across the Karelian Isthmus were III Corps (Lieutenant-General Hjalmar Siilasvuo) by Lake Ladoga and IV Corps (Lieutenant-General Taavetti 'Pappa' Laatikainen) by the Gulf of Finland. The forces around Kuuterselkä consisted of 3. Division (Major-General Aaro Pajari) made up of II. Battalion, Jalkaväkirykmentti 53 (Infantry Regiment 53, hereafter II./JR 53), I./JR 48 and Erillinen Pataljoona 13 (Separate Battalion 13). A battlegroup under Colonel Albert Puroma consisted of the *Jäger* Brigade and two *Tykistöryhmät* (TykRH, 'artillery groups'). The *Jäger* Brigade was composed of Jääkäripataljoona 2 ('Jäger Battalion 2', hereafter JP 2), JP 3, JP 4, a *Panssarijääkäripataljoona* ('Armoured Battalion'), the 1st Company of the *Rynnäkkötykkipataljoona* (1./RynTykP, 'Assault Gun Battalion') which had 11 StuG III assault guns, and a *Panssari-ilmatorjuntapatteri* ('armoured anti-aircraft battery'). The two *Tykistöryhmät* were named after their commanders: TykRH 'Nuolimaa' with four heavy batteries of 150–155mm howitzers, 47 pieces in all, and TykRH 'Hankipohja' with one heavy battery (RaskPsto 16) and a field-gun battery from KTR 9.

A Red Army KV-1S heavy tank advances with accompanying infantry, sometime in 1943–44. Though the T-34-76 and T-34-85 medium tanks provided the backbone of the Red Army's armoured forces, heavy tanks still had an important role to play in spearheading assaults and initiating breakthroughs of the enemy's main line of defence. The KV-1S retained the 76mm M1941 ZiS-5 gun but it was lighter and more manoeuvrable than earlier KV variants, at the cost of thinner armour. The bold three-digit numbering on the tank's turret likely designates the vehicle's company, platoon and individual tank number, though such markings were not always consistent, with different units employing their own systems of identification. (Courtesy of the Central Museum of the Armed Forces, Moscow via Stavka)

1 0700hrs, 14 June: The Soviet attack on Kuuterselkä begins with a 74-minute bombardment followed by a combined-arms attack at 0830hrs. The lone Finnish battalion defending the village, II./JR 53, is soon overwhelmed.

2 Midday, 14 June: Kuuterselkä is captured by infantry from the 133rd Rifle Regiment and other Soviet units who fight off Finnish counter-attacks. An attempted exploitation by the 14th Rifle Regiment towards Liikola is checked by I./JR 48.

3 2245hrs, 14 June: A more substantial Finnish counter-attack involving three battalions of *Jäger* with support from the StuG IIIs of 1./RynTykP and two artillery groups is launched, recapturing the northern side of Kuuterselkä in the face of stiff resistance by the early hours of 15 June.

4 0700hrs, 15 June: The Finnish counter-attack is halted in the face of insurmountable Soviet resistance. By 1045hrs the *Jäger* and assault guns are withdrawn.

Battlefield environment

Kuuterselkä was on the VT-Line, around 10km to the south-west of the town of Kivennapa which sat astride one of the few roads that connected Leningrad with Viipuri, the main objective of Cherepanov's 23rd Army. The ground on the approach to Kuuterselkä was heavily forested with a number of lakes and swamps (for example, Lake Kuuterselänjärvi 1km to the west of the town) adding to the terrain's challenging nature for armoured forces, though there were some open fields around Kuuterselkä itself. A country road ran from the coast north-east through the town and on towards Kivennapa, with a junction at Kuuterselkä branching northwards to the village of Liikola on the shores of Lake Suulajärvi. Some 5km to the west a railway line ran in a north-westerly direction, connected to Raivola by a spur and passing through Sahakylä, Mustamäki and Korpikylä by Lake Kanneljärvi. The local defences at Kuuterselkä were relatively modest, consisting in large part of infantry shelters (low log-lined trenches with covered areas) studded with machine-gun bunkers, a few of which were reinforced. Bunkers were of earth-and-log construction, and lines of rudimentary anti-tank obstacles in the shape of large deliberately half-buried boulders were also sited on open ground around Kuuterselkä.

A local dwelling pressed into service as temporary accommodation for Finnish troops arriving at Vammelsuu–Kuuterselkä in advance of the Soviet attack, the photograph being taken on 18 May 1944. Finnish preparations for the coming attack were generally poor: their main defensive lines – the VT and VKT – were unfinished and generally too weak even where they were complete, and little thought had gone into properly reinforcing the Finnish units that were stationed on the front line. There was a dearth of infrastructure available to accommodate any increase in military activity, or to provide longer-term secure shelter for the area's defenders. (SA-kuva 151026)

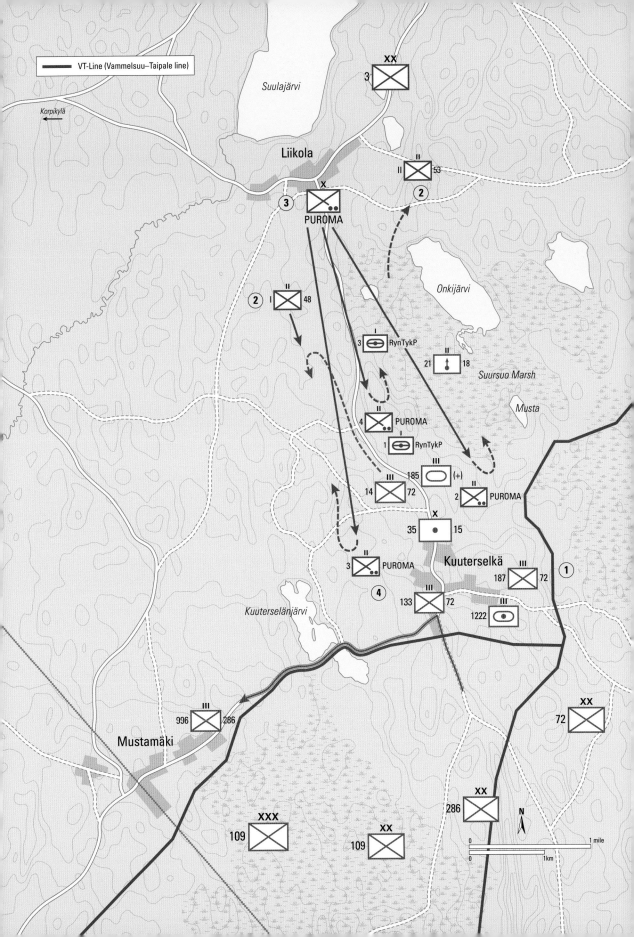

VT-Line (Vammelsuu–Taipale line)

Suulajärvi

← *Korpikylä*

3 XX ☒

Liikola

II II ☒ 53 **2**

3 X ☒ •• PUROMA

Onkijärvi

2 I II ☒ 48

I 3 ⟐ RynTykP

II 21 ♦ 18 *Suursuo Marsh*

Musta

II 4 ☒ •• PUROMA

1 ⟐ RynTykP

III 185 ▭ (+)

III 14 ☒ 72

II 2 ☒ •• PUROMA

X 35 ▪ 15

II 3 ☒ •• PUROMA

4

Kuuterselänjärvi

Kuuterselkä

III 187 ☒ 72 **1**

III 133 ☒ 72

III 1222 ▭

III 996 ☒ 286

Mustamäki

72 XX ☒

286 XX ☒

XXX 109 ☒

XX 109 ☒

N ↑

0   1 mile
0   1km

INTO COMBAT

The bombs began to fall at 0700hrs on 9 June, the first of an uncountable number delivered by a VVS bomber force over 1,000 aircraft strong. The air attacks were complemented by an enormous bombardment from hundreds of guns, including some huge siege pieces that had been allocated just for the occasion. All along the front line and for some kilometres back Soviet bombs and shells pounded into Finnish positions, disrupting lines of communication, destroying many forward observation posts and neutralizing minefields. By the evening Soviet probes had begun to dig at the ragged Finnish border in front of 10. Division to see if there were gaps big enough to exploit, but the Finnish line held. The shelling carried on throughout the night, suddenly increasing in intensity at 0420hrs on 10 June before ceasing abruptly at 0500hrs – the ground attack had commenced.

Estimates about the intensity of the Soviet preparatory bombardment have varied greatly, with the Soviet military historian M. Frolov calculating that on 10 June the Soviet artillery fired 354,000 shells into the Rajajoki–Valkeasaari area, the heaviest bombardment of the war so far. By contrast, the defending 10. Division's two artillery regiments could only return 3,700 shells of their own (Nenye 2016: 201). The guns had done their work, and the armoured spearheads leading the infantry of the 63rd Guards Rifle and 54th Rifle divisions stormed through the Finnish line with relative ease. Unlike in 1939 this was an operation for which the Soviet units had trained extensively, using similar terrain and detailed planning to ensure that their rehearsals were accurate. Broken by the relentlessness and power of the Soviet artillery, 10. Division mostly melted away as soon as the fire let up, while 2. Division was shunted aside with little effort.

The Finnish Army's centre of command was too far behind the front, resulting in confusion as to the size and nature of the Soviet attack and a sluggish response to what was an emergency of the first order. The seriousness of the situation became clearer as the day wore on, but attempts at timely reinforcement were difficult to organize in part because the reserves had been held too far behind the lines. Despite the unmistakable signs of a build-up in the preceding weeks, the Finnish intelligence services had missed all sense of what was about to happen, a situation exacerbated by the distributed command structure between army- and corps-level headquarters and the lack of a dedicated Karelian 'Theatre Command', despite it being the most likely place that the Soviets would strike. The resulting fiasco saw the Soviet forces able to expand their bridgehead with relative ease and speed in the first critical days of the campaign. By 13 June the Red Army's armoured spearheads had enjoyed a brief rest and were now ready to push on and assault a weak point on the VT-Line at Kuuterselkä.

The Finnish position was desperate. There was only a single battalion – II./JR 53 (Major Aito Keravuori) – in position along the VT-Line defences at Kuuterselkä, with the supporting battalions of 3. Division 5km further back. More substantial reinforcements in the shape of the *Panssaridivisioona*'s *Jäger* Brigade and some supporting armour were on the way, but it was doubtful they would arrive before the Red Army did. At 0700hrs on 14 June that question was answered when a quick and vicious artillery bombardment thundered

Mikhail Danilovich Grishin

Mikhail Danilovich Grishin was born into a peasant family in 1898 in the Tula region. Initially working as an agricultural labourer, he was wounded while fighting in the Baltic region during World War I, joining the Red Army in 1918. He served in the Russian Civil War (1918–21) and rose steadily through the ranks during the inter-war years, achieving the rank of colonel and command of the 2nd Rifle Division by November 1939. The invasion of the Soviet Union found him on holiday, but he quickly returned, taking part in the defence of Borisov at the end of June 1941; he commanded the 4th Airborne Corps in the battles for Krichev, and later the 6th Rifle Division during its

defensive battles in Byelorussia and the Bryansk region, as well as the battles for the liberation of Voronezh in 1942. From 1943 to 1944 he commanded first the 376th Rifle Division and then the 286th Rifle Division in raising the siege of Leningrad. He continued to lead the 286th Rifle Division during the breakthrough of the VT-Line, moving with his division to the 1st Ukrainian Front in 1945 where he participated in the Vistula–Oder operation and conducted offensive battles for Kraków, Katowice, and the Dombrowski Coal Basin in Silesia. After the war he transferred to the Reserves in 1946, eventually dying in Moscow on 14 April 1982.

down on the VT-Line positions around Kuuterselkä, lifting at 0825hrs to allow the advance of the 109th Rifle Corps' three rifle divisions, with the 109th Rifle Division and the 1st Red Banner Tank Brigade advancing on the western flank along the railway line, the 286th Rifle Division in the centre (on the west side of the main road) and the 72nd Rifle Division to the east of the road. The main assault was led by the 185th and 98th Separate Tank regiments (T-34 medium tanks plus T-60 and T-70 light tanks) and elements from the 1222nd Self-Propelled Gun Regiment (SU-76 self-propelled guns) followed by the 14th Rifle Regiment (Lieutenant-Colonel Vasili I. Korolev) and the 133rd Rifle Regiment (Major Koliuch), both from the 72nd Rifle Division, and the 994th Rifle Regiment from the 286th Rifle Division. As soon as the Soviet attack began to develop, Major-General Aaro Pajari ordered I./JR 48 forward to reinforce II./JR 53, but the speed and weight of the Soviet assault, buoyed up by its armour, smashed its way through the Finnish positions in a matter of hours, sometimes knocking out bunkers at point-blank range with anti-tank guns, and capturing Kuuterselkä by midday.

Finnish attempts to force back the Soviet tank and rifle regiments were thrown off with relative ease, the paucity of Finnish reserves meaning that it was all Pajari could do to try to patch his ruptured line until he received

Albert Puroma

Albert Aleksander Puroma was born on 21 February 1895 in Tuusula near Finland's southern coast. He came from a modest family and first made a living as a sailor, but World War I saw him interned by Germany as an enemy alien (Finland was still under Russian control at the time). Rather than spend his time as an internee, Puroma volunteered for the Königlich-Preußischen Jäger-Bataillon Nr. 27, a unit manned by Finns that fought for Germany; he was accepted into the regiment's 2. Kompagnie on 6 November 1915, fighting on the Eastern Front. Joining the new Finnish Army on 11 February 1918, he quickly secured the command of

a company in Jääkärirykmentti 4 (*Jäger* Regiment 4) during the Finnish Civil War. Puroma participated in the Winter War under the command of Lieutenant-General Harald Öhquist in the Second Army District of Viipuri and later as head of the Kannas Military District. Upon the outbreak of the Continuation War he became commander of 6. Division, fighting at Kiestinki and Louhivaara and eventually gaining command of the armoured division's *Jäger* Brigade. His battlegroup fought at Kuuterselkä and Vuosalmi, continuing his service into the Lapland War. He resigned from the Finnish Army on 29 February 1956 and died in Helsinki on 8 April 1987.

reinforcements or the order to retreat. The Soviets, now fully in control of Kuuterselkä and its immediate environs, went about fortifying their new prize: the 133rd Rifle Regiment plus elements of the 286th Rifle Division secured the village; the 286th Rifle Division's 996th Rifle Regiment struck out to the south-west, capturing Mustamäki and its railway station and then sending the regiment's 1st Battalion ever further up the line in the direction of Korpikylä; and the 14th Rifle Regiment advanced out of Kuuterselkä in the direction of Liikola, where it was checked by a counter-attack from I./JR 48.

At IV Corps headquarters, Lieutenant-General Laatikainen, faced with the imminent collapse of the VT-Line if the hole at Kuuterselkä could not be plugged, decided to try to rescue the situation by using reinforcements that were just arriving in the area that afternoon to launch an altogether more serious counter-attack, one intended to recapture Kuuterselkä and the Finnish forward defences to its south. The task fell to Colonel Puroma, commander of the *Jäger* Brigade, whose three battalions would be supported in the attempt by two artillery groups and a company of assault guns in an ad hoc force known as Taisteluosasto *Puroma* (Battlegroup *Puroma*). JP 3 would form the western (right) flank of the attack, with the central assault group consisting of JP 4 supported by the StuG IIIs of 1./RynTykP, while JP 2 would advance on the eastern (left) flank. The operation would begin at nightfall. The Soviets, well aware that an attack likely supported by armour was forming, organized their defences. The northern approach to Kuuterselkä was defended by the 14th Rifle Regiment, with the 133rd Rifle Regiment to its left and the 187th Rifle Regiment to its right, with the 1222nd Self-Propelled Gun Regiment in reserve. In addition, the T-34s of the 185th Separate Tank Regiment were bolstered by a company of T-34-85s from the 98th Separate Tank Regiment and five IS-2s detailed from two Guards heavy-tank units (Zaloga 2019: 63–64).

The Finnish counter-attack began a little after night had fallen at 2245hrs on 14 June. In the centre V. Rautiainen, an orderly in 1./JP 4, recalled how his medical section led by Under-Sergeant Kari (a Helsinki man) set off from the vicinity of Liikola towards Kuuterselkä barely 2km away, walking through the trees on either side of the road while the assault guns of Captain Carl-Birger Kvikant's 1./RynTykP trundled along the roadway under a cloudy but dry sky. As the lead elements of Taisteluosasto *Puroma* neared the thinning edge of the forest the assault guns moved off the road and formed a line, behind which the infantry followed; the Soviets of the 14th Rifle Regiment held their fire until the Finns began to move out of the trees into the clear ground before the village, where their infantry and tanks opened up. A quick and intense battle ensued in which fire from the Finnish assault guns played havoc with the lead tanks of the 185th Separate Tank Regiment, whose crews seemed to be caught off-guard by their opponents despite the earlier intelligence warnings. The combined effect of the Finnish assault guns and the accompanying *Jäger* soon forced the 185th Separate Tank Regiment's T-34s and the 14th Rifle Regiment's infantry companies to fall back towards the village. As the Finns moved forward Rautiainen was surprised that he did not see any destroyed Finnish or Soviet armour because both sides seemed to have been hammering away

at each other constantly – though in fact at least three Soviet tanks had been knocked out in that first encounter. As Rautiainen's company pushed ahead a 'Sotka' (the Finnish nickname for the T-34) surprised them, moving in to attack. At first, Rautiainen wasn't sure what sort of tank it was, other than its smaller size and gun meant it could not be a KV; that proved to be something of a moot point as the tank, responding to the rifle and pistol fire with which Rautiainen's company had engaged it, sped towards them only to lose its tracks trying to drive over felled trees, its crew subsequently abandoning the stricken vehicle (Rautiainen 1962: 264).

The advance of JP 4 bypassed the 211th Mortar Regiment (Lieutenant-Colonel Georgi M. Shepelev) that had supported the 109th Rifle Division during the day's action and which had set up its 120mm mortars at the edge of the Suursuo Marsh. Cut off from friendly forces, Shepelev quickly organized his regiment in a circular 'hedgehog' defence, aided by the arrival of stragglers with anti-tank guns and a couple of T-34s as well. Shepelev wasn't content to sit and wait for the Finns to come for him, launching three separate counter-attacks through the night, but all were repulsed. For their part the Finns did not have the resources to deal with Shepelev, and instead concentrated on moving forward against Kuuterselkä. Shortly before midnight, 3./RynTykP (Captain Tor Kumlin) began to move towards Taisteluosasto *Puroma* to provide additional support in what was becoming a rather difficult fight. A little more than half an hour later, at 0030hrs on 15 June, the lead elements of JP 4 with its supporting assault guns reached the northern perimeter of Kuuterselkä. They could not make it much further.

Meanwhile, over on the western flank as JP 3 began to form up before its attack against the positions held by the 133rd Rifle Regiment, a continuous rain of light-artillery shellfire began to fall, peppering the Finnish battalion and causing it some casualties as well as a certain degree of confusion in the ranks. Nevertheless JP 3's companies began to advance through the heavily wooded terrain, 1./JP 3 to the left of a simple country road and 3./JP 3 to its right, both making good progress, pushing the soldiers of the 133rd Rifle Regiment back towards Kuuterselkä. The waves of Soviet artillery shells

ABOVE LEFT
Finnish soldiers shelter in a log bunker on the VT-Line (Vammelsuu–Taipale), 16 June 1944. The soldier to the fore grips a later-model KP/-31 with its prominent SJR (*suujarru*, 'muzzle brake') clearly visible, while behind him one compatriot toys with the knurled fuze cap of a *varsikranaatti* m/32 (the belt clip on the charge distinguishing it from the later m/41 pattern) and the other manhandles what appears to be a Finnish m/32–33 Maxim machine gun. (SA-kuva 143060)

ABOVE RIGHT
Commanded by 2nd Lieutenant Olli Aulanko, this 'Sturmi' (StuG III) of the *Panssaridivisioona* saw action at Kuuterselkä, knocking out one IS-2 and one KV heavy tank and three T-34 medium tanks in the battle. The *Rynnäkkötykkipataljoona* acquitted itself well during the battle, mainly due to the experience of its crews, their knowledge of the local terrain, and the better situational awareness provided by the StuG III's sighting equipment and radio systems (Zaloga 2019: 75). (SA-kuva 156192)

were now coming thick and fast, making movement difficult and reliable communication even more so, but it was possible to avoid the worst of it: as they pursued the retreating Soviet infantry the Finns were hugging them so closely that much of the enemy artillery fire overshot, dropping harmlessly behind the attackers. The Soviet tanks were clearly visible but they kept to the road, and so as long as the Finns manoeuvred through the forests the Soviet armour caused them few problems. The enemy infantry, however, proved much more dogged, aided by a low fog that had arisen in the early hours of the night, enveloping the maze of trees and dense undergrowth. Finding the enemy proved difficult and dangerous, with more than one veteran soldier wounded in Soviet hand-grenade attacks that materialized out of the mist.

Toio V. Hyvönen, a member of JP 3, recalled that by the time his unit arrived at the secondary positions of the VT-Line on the outskirts of Kuuterselkä the worst of the artillery bombardment seemed to have passed. The men of the battalion had heard the thunderous shelling of 9 July all too clearly, and later that same evening Hyvönen's company, 1./JP 3, had been ordered (along with the rest of the battalion) to move out on their bicycles in full kit (Hyvönen 1975: 192). That bombardment had been many kilometres distant but its strength had been unmistakable, and it was a harbinger of what was to come.

As the Finns pushed on the Soviet resistance grew ever-more serious. By dawn (around 0300hrs), JP 3 had reached the northern edge of Kuuterselkä's village square. Hyvönen remembered how it seemed like it was just then that the devil unleashed his wrath. Artillery shells of every calibre started raining down, while dozens of ground-attack aircraft appeared with the light and constantly strafed the Finnish line, which was withering as a result. Men were breaking under the strain of the Soviet attack, men who had not seen any significant action for over two years and who as a result were losing their

Red Army riflemen on the attack in 1944. According to the updated 'Regulation for the Rifle Troops of the Red Army', issued in November 1942, during an assault the squad leader was supposed to keep all members of his unit in sight at all times, coordinating their actions. The rifle squad's LMG was meant to open fire when within 800m of the objective, with crack riflemen joining in from 600m, ordinary riflemen at 400m and SMGs at 100–200m. The last 40–50m of the attack was supposed to be conducted as a charge, light-machine-gunners firing from the hip and all the troops shouting war cries as they went (Sharp 1995: 103–04). (Sovfoto/Universal Images Group via Getty Images)

nerve in the face of such an intense barrage of enemy fire. Many simply broke, running back to the relative safety of the support lines or the cover of the forest. The battalion commander, Lieutenant-Colonel Jouko Hynninen, detailed his second-in-command, Onni Laitinen, to go and gather up all the men he could find who had fallen back towards the support line and bring them back. Hyvönen saw how the soldiers who had not given in to cowardice before were broken by the terrible drumming of shellfire which pushed otherwise decent men into abandoning their positions. One *Jäger* from Hyvönen's own unit asked that he be allowed to return to the rear, so great was his fear of staying in the teeth of the Soviet attack. The man was shaking like a hollow reed so Hyvönen told him that he could go and be wherever he wanted, but as bad luck would have it sometime later he was killed by a hand grenade, even though he was in the supposed safety of the support line (Hyvönen 1975: 193).

Hyvönen's platoon leader had been wounded, so the second-in-command Hyvönen took over the 3rd Platoon – a difficult job considering the stress of the situation and the fact that men from different platoons and companies were becoming intermixed in the confusion of the fight. Despite such problems the Finns continued to inch forward as the Soviets fell back towards their main line of defence, a series of works that were first made by the Finns as they faced in the direction of the enemy. All the time the Soviet artillery fire was increasing, as were strafing and bombing runs by ground-attack aircraft, but by making their way from one infantry slit trench to another the Finns managed to drive the enemy out of the position, capturing a hastily abandoned battery of field artillery in the process. Hyvönen's men attempted to turn the guns on their former owners but there weren't enough of them – he only had a handful of his platoon with him in the gun pits – and what was more worrying was the fact that there did not appear to be any *Jäger* to his left, even though he knew that 2nd Lieutenant Ilkama's platoon ought to be occupying similar captured fighting positions.

One of Hyvönen's men was wounded by a shell splinter despite sheltering in a foxhole at around the same time that Hyvönen noticed the enemy starting to flank his position several hundred metres off to the west, but he assumed that his platoon was safe because his battalion's 3rd Company (3./JP 3) should have been covering that approach. The battering of the Soviet artillery continued, with no apparent reply from the Finnish guns, something that may have contributed to what Hyvönen saw next. Ilkama's platoon had finally appeared on his left, but it was retreating, leaving Hyvönen's small force without infantry on his immediate flank and no apparent artillery support likely in the event of an enemy attack. He did not realize it at the time but his and Ilkama's platoons had reached further than any other unit in JP 3 or the rest of the brigade. The position was untenable and Hyvönen ordered his men to pull back, rushing through the village square amid the falling artillery shells, taking up the position they had reached earlier that same morning. There were quite a few *Jäger* from the rest of the battalion in the same spot, some of whom informed him that both of 1./JP 3's company officers, Lieutenant Inkinen and Lieutenant Kantanen, had been killed near the road during the advance.

RIGHT
A portrait of Lance Corporal Veikko Leppäkoski, taken at Noskuanselkä on 7 July 1944. During the opening stages of the engagement at Kuuterselkä on 12 June Leppäkoski was credited with destroying three KV heavy tanks and six T-34 medium tanks with his 7.5cm PaK 40 anti-tank gun, his actions later seeing him promoted to *alikersantti* ('under-sergeant'). (SA-kuva 156176)

FAR RIGHT
A portrait of a Soviet *razvedchik* ('scout') on patrol, armed with a PPS-43 SMG and wearing an 'amoeba'-pattern camouflage smock. Scouts played an increasingly important role as the Continuation War progressed, with artillery scouts infiltrating behind the lines to observe targets and control fire, and infantry scouts providing ground reconnaissance of enemy dispositions at the battalion and regimental level. Such units planned and practised their proposed missions, were staffed with the most competent and suitable men, and were provided with the best weapons and communications equipment available. (Courtesy of the Central Museum of the Armed Forces, Moscow via Stavka)

Captain Arvo Kuukka was there too and was none too pleased to see Hyvönen, accusing him of abandoning his position and thus exposing the flank of 3./JP 3 on the right. Hyvönen replied that the only soldiers he had actually seen on his right were Red Army men, not Finns. Without further ado Kuukka organized the *Jäger* around him, including those of Hyvönen's platoon, into a composite force that moved forward once again, using the same cover and foxholes to advance back to the twice-abandoned line (Hyvönen 1975: 193). The intensity of the Soviet artillery fire had not diminished at all, and there was nothing the Finns could do to push ahead any further – they lacked the men, the tanks and the artillery to force the Soviets to relinquish Kuuterselkä. JP 3 had penetrated further than any other unit, but it was too small and had suffered too many casualties to hold its tenuous gains. JP 2 had not made much headway until the same problems forced it back on its heels, and despite the initial success of JP 4 and its accompanying assault guns the central Finnish thrust had also run out of steam. The assault guns had proved themselves invaluable in dealing with Soviet armour but when they ran into an entire artillery brigade (the 35th, from the 15th Artillery Division) that deployed across the road just ahead of the Finns and began bombarding them with 122mm shells, all further progress by the assault guns and JP 4 ground to a halt.

In spite of the dedication of men like Kuukka it was clear enough to Puroma and those above him that further success was impossible. All too soon at 0700hrs the order to fall back was given again, this time for good. Captain Kuukka was killed during those last hours, with many others sharing his fate or being wounded – 236 men in all from JP 3, by far the worst losses suffered by any of the *Jäger* battalions. A day or two later, in a review of JP 3's actions during the battle, its commander, Lieutenant-Colonel Hynninen, praised many of the men for their courage in obeying orders and completing the tasks assigned to them, but when addressing those who had fallen back to the support line in the face of Soviet air and artillery attacks, his voice grew tight and he asked them where they were while many of their comrades fulfilled their military oaths down to the last breath (Hyvönen 1975: 193).

Tali–Ihantala

21–30 June 1944

BACKGROUND TO BATTLE

With a hole punched through the VT-Line by the Soviet 109th Rifle Corps, the Finns of Lieutenant-General Taavetti Laatikainen's IV Corps found themselves in a fighting retreat, with all attempts to slow the Soviet advance thwarted by further repeated breakthroughs and armoured exploitations of Finnish defences. On 14 June Lieutenant-General Lennart Oesch had been given command of III and IV Corps – effectively all the Finnish troops on the Karelian Isthmus – but there was little he could do in the immediate term to stem the Soviet flow. On 15 June Soviet armoured formations made the most of the hole they had torn in the Finnish lines at Kuuterselkä by looping around to the south-west, catching *Jäger* Major-General Lars Melander's *Ratsuväkiprikaati* in the rear at Vammeljärvi, forcing him to pull back and in the process making the rest of the VT-Line untenable. A day later and to the north, Siilasvuo's III Corps began to fall backs from the southern bank of the

A pair of Soviet SU-122 self-propelled assault guns fight their way through the dense undergrowth and close forest that dominated so much of the Karelian landscape. The SU-122 (*Samokhodnaya Ustanovka*, 'self-propelled unit') carried a 122mm M-30S howitzer as its main armament on a converted T-34 chassis. SU-122s were organized into *Samokhodno-Artilleriyskogo Polki* ('medium self-propelled artillery regiments') of 18 vehicles each: a command element of one T-34 medium tank and one BA-64 armoured car, plus four batteries with four SU-122s each. The SU-122 began to be replaced with the better-balanced 85mm SU-85 self-propelled assault gun in September 1943, with most SU-122s continuing to operate through late 1943 and 1944 until they were no longer serviceable or destroyed in combat. (Nik Cornish at www.stavka.org.uk)

Vuoksi River, a move which, taken in conjunction with the poor state of many of the heavily mauled units of IV Corps which were unable to pull together coherent or effective counter-attacks, led Mannerheim to direct a general retreat to the VKT-Line. His daily orders on 19 June 1944 demanded that it was here that the Finnish Army would stand and fight, engaging in stark defensive combat despite his frank admission that the line's fortifications were either non-existent or had barely begun to be formed. He had confidence in his men, their ability to make the most of the terrain, and their *sisu*, a particularly Finnish term describing a form of grim stoic resolution in the face of hard odds (Nenye 2016: 217–18).

The rifle corps of Colonel-General Gusev's 21st Army pressed on eagerly, snatching Viipuri from Finnish hands in barely a single day of fighting on 20 June. The shock of Viipuri's rapid fall caused the Finns to send out diplomatic feelers to gauge whether the Soviets would be receptive to a negotiated peace, but the Stavka would accept nothing less than unconditional surrender, with all the bleak consequences such an abject move would entail. The Soviet conditions were rejected out of hand, Mannerheim concentrating all his focus on the VKT-Line; the defensive positions were primarily being filled by troops retreating in the face of the Soviet advance, but soon also by Finnish reserves that were starting to arrive at the front. There was something of a scramble to ensure that the VKT-Line would hold. Siilasvuo's III Corps held the north-eastern stretch from Vuoksi to Taipale on Lake Ladoga, Laatikainen's IV Corps was centred on the area between Vuoksi and Viipuri, while the newly arriving V Corps (*Jäger* Major-General Antero Svensson) took up position in the area behind Viipuri from Tienhaara along the western coastline, their job being to stop any Soviet attempts to outflank the VKT-Line by crossing Viipuri Bay.

Suomenvedenpohja Bay, a narrow body of water 9km long, ran north-east from Viipuri, and it was on its eastern bank that the VKT-Line was anchored, with 3. Prikaati ('3rd Brigade', also known as the 'Blue Brigade', Colonel Lauri Haanterä) holding the position. To the east of 3. Prikaati to Lake Leitimojärvi was 18. Division – led by Major-General Paavo Paalu until 29 June, then Colonel Otto Gustaf Snellman – fielding JR 6, JR 27, JR 48, KTR 19 and RaskPsto 26 ('Heavy Battery 26'). The line between lakes Leitimojärvi and Näätälänjärvi was held by *Jäger* Major-General Pietari Autti's 4. Division, composed of JR 5, JR 25, JR 46, KTR 1 and RaskPsto 26. Commanded by *Jäger* Major-General Ruben Lagus, the *Suomen Panssaridivisioona* ('Finnish Armoured Division') was being held in reserve; it included Puroma's *Jääkäriprikaati* and Colonel Sven Björkman's *Panssariprikaati* ('Tank Brigade'). Further Finnish reinforcements were arriving in the shape of Major-General Einar Vihma's 6. Division (JR 12, JR 33, JR 54 and KTR 14), Major-General Alonzo Sundman's 17. Division (JR 13, JR 34, JR 61 and KTR 8) and – from 27 June onwards – Colonel Kaarlo Heiskanen's 11. Division (JR 8, JR 29, JR 50, KTR 4 and RaskPsto 30).

When he first saw the scale of the Soviet attack, Mannerheim called upon Germany for assistance on 12–13 June, with almost immediate results. Finland's modest air capability at Tali–Ihantala consisted of Lieutenant-Colonel Gustaf Magnusson's Lentorykmentti 3 (LeR 3, 'Air Regiment 3') – 33 Messerschmitt Bf 109 and 18 Brewster Model 239 fighters, and a

single Fokker C.X biplane – and Colonel Olavi Sarko's LeR 4 – 33 Bristol Blenheim, 12 Junkers Ju 88 and eight Dornier Do 17Z bombers – but thanks to Mannerheim's request help was on the way. Arriving in Finland on 16 June, Gefechtsverband *Kuhlmey* (a 'battlegroup' named for its commander, Oberstleutnant Kurt Kuhlmey) would be thrown into the defensive battles around Viipuri and Tali–Ihantala, racking up over 3,000 sorties before the end of July. It consisted of a mixed Luftwaffe unit of 60–70 aircraft from I./Schlachtgeschwader 3 (33 Junkers Ju 87D-5 'Stuka' dive-bombers), II./Jagdgeschwader 54 (62 Focke-Wulf Fw 190A-6 fighters from Estonia), I./Schlachtgeschwader 5 (16 Fw 190F-3 and F-8 fighter-bombers from Alakurtti), elements of Nahaufklärergruppe 5 (eight Messerschmitt Bf 109G-8 reconnaissance aircraft), and support from Transportmaschinengruppe 10 (35 Savoia-Marchetti SM.81/AR transport aircraft). Further German assistance would materialize on 22 June with the landing of Hauptmann Hans-Wilhelm Cardeneo's Sturmgeschütz-Brigade 303, with 22 StuG III Ausf G assault guns and nine Sturmhaubitze 42 assault howitzers; the unit would arrive at the front by 27 June.

The advancing Soviet forces, unaware of the rapid Finnish build-up, were characterized by a slight touch of understandable hubris. Their success in the opening days of the campaign had been unquestionable: after the initial breakthrough they had cracked the VT-Line in short order and passed over the old Mannerheim Line without encountering any resistance, finally capturing Viipuri right on schedule – a suitable capstone to the operation's first phase. The Stavka assumed that the freshly promoted Marshal Leonid Alexandrovich Govorov's Leningrad Front would continue to progress apace, and made no move to reinforce the 21st and 23rd armies in their new operations against the VKT-Line, partly because they seemed to be doing well enough with what they had, and also because Operation *Bagration* was just about to start on 23 June. The overall plan for the Leningrad Front was for Gusev's 21st Army to breach the VKT-Line just to the west of Viipuri, after which it would swing westwards and make for Miehikkälä, while Korovnikov's 59th Army would follow behind in a second wave and branch off north-west to Lappeenranta; to Gusev's east Cherepanov's 23rd Army would attack through the centre and drive north to Imatra and on north-east to Hiitola by the shores of Lake Ladoga. If the past ten days' fighting were any indication, Helsinki would soon be within reach.

MAP KEY

1   21–24 June: In the wake of Viipuri's fall, Colonel-General Gusev's 21st Army begins the next stage of its offensive, attempting to break through the incomplete VKT-Line. The rifle divisions of the 97th and 109th Rifle corps make some hard-fought progress, but there is no breakthrough.

2   25 June: A significant new Soviet attempt to punch a hole through the Finnish positions is launched by multiple divisions of the 21st Army, with the lead being taken by the 45th and 64th Guards Rifle divisions of the 30th Guards Rifle Corps. Initial Soviet successes on either side of Lake Leitimojärvi are checked by the Finns, but a narrow salient remains in Soviet hands.

3   27 June: A major three-pronged Finnish counter-attack on Kuusela and Aniskala, led by armoured elements of the Suomen Panssaridivisioona, 18. Division and the *Jäger*

battalions, attempts to cut off the two leading Soviet Guards divisions (63rd and 64th) and form a *motti*. The attacking Finnish forces are not strong enough to close the noose, however, and both Soviet divisions remain in contact with the rest of the 21st Army.

4   28 June: A major Soviet attempt to break out of the salient at multiple points spoils the Finnish plans for another counter-attack and threatens to destabilize the entire Finnish position.

5   Midnight, 29/30 June: Lieutenant-General Oesch takes the decision to call off any further counter-attacks and draw back all Finnish units to a shorter and more defensible line running from Vakkila to Ihantala. Fighting will continue in the succeeding weeks, but the Soviets will make no further significant progress in the Karelian Isthmus.

Battlefield environment

The VKT-Line was in an even worse state of readiness than the VT-Line, with work on it only beginning after the new year, and that on a decidedly modest section near Viipuri (Johansen 2016: 275). Despite the poor state of the VKT-Line the landscape to the north-west of Viipuri was more suitable for defensive combat; the open spaces that had given Soviet armoured formations room to breathe in the first ten days of their advance narrowed, hemmed in by boreal forest, higher rocky ground and numerous lakes. There was one small 10km-wide corridor to the east of Viipuri that still offered some

prospect for armoured forces to make their mark, from Tali, a small town that sat between the lakes of Leitimojärvi and Repolanjärvi, to Ihantala about 6km to the north. The main railway line ran north-west from Viipuri through Tienhaara and eventually to Helsinki, but a branch line ran 5km north-east through Tali on to the western side of Lake Kokkoselkä and finally Lake Ladoga. There were two main roadways, one from Viipuri running north-east to Ihantala, the other running north-west from Tali to Juustila; the two roads crossed at what would become a vital junction, Portinhoikka.

A photograph of the Ihantala Road taken on 26 June 1944. What appears to be a destroyed Soviet ISU-122 assault gun can just be made out in the middle of the roadway. The ISU-122 (not to be confused with the SU-122) was a new weapon, only leaving the factory in April 1944; it was a combination of the ISU-152's chassis with the A19C 122mm gun (the A19 was also used in the M1931/37 field gun; the 'C' indicated that the gun had been modified for installation on a self-propelled mount). The ISU-122 and its later variant, the ISU-122S (from August 1944), along with the SU-152 and ISU-152, were formed into *Otdel'nykh tyazholykh samokhodno-artilleriyskikh polkakh* (OTSAP, 'separate heavy self-propelled artillery regiments'). From May 1943 to 1945, 53 such units were formed, each equipped with 21 self-propelled guns in four batteries of five vehicles, plus the self-propelled gun of the regiment commander. (SA-kuva 152246)

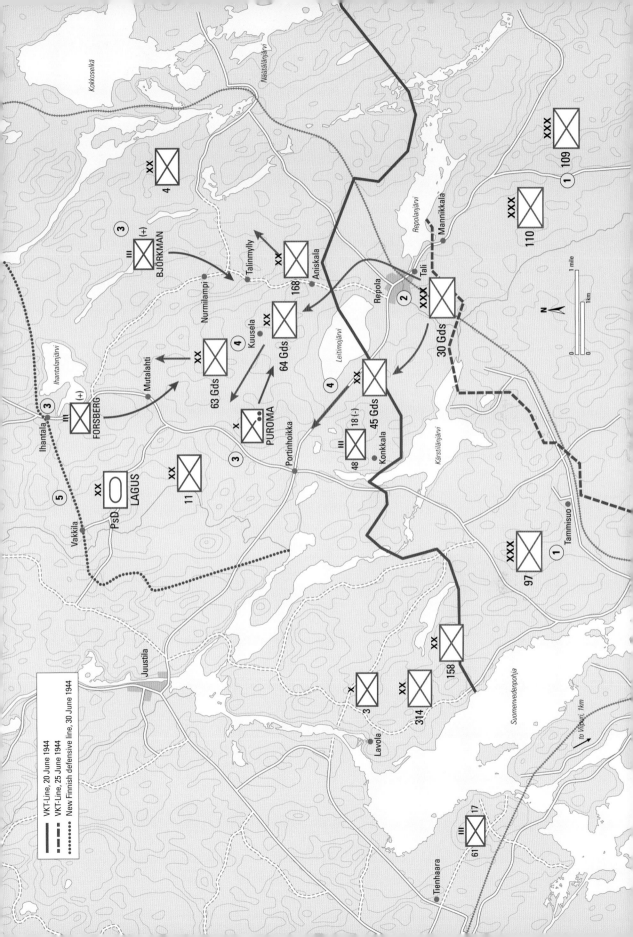

Kokkoselkä

Näätälänjärvi

XXX
109
1

XXX
110

XX
4

3
III (+)
BJÖRKMAN

Talinmylly

XX
168
Aniskala

Repolanjärvi

Mannikkala

Tali

XXX
30 Gds
2

1 mile

N

1km

Nurmilampi

XX
64 Gds
Kuusela
4

XX
63 Gds
Mutalahti

Repola

Leitimojärvi

Ihantalanjärvi

3
III (+)
FORSBERG

x
PUROMA
Portinhoikka
3

III
48
18 (-)
Konkkala
45 Gds
XX
4

Kärstiiänjärvi

Ihantala
3

5

XX
PsD
LAGUS

XX
11

Vakkila

Juustila

XXX
97
1
Tammisuo

x
3
Lavola

XX
314

XX
158

Suomenvedenpohja

III
61
17
Tienhaara

to Viipuri, 1km

VKT-Line, 20 June 1944

VKT-Line, 25 June 1944

New Finnish defensive line, 30 June 1944

INTO COMBAT

A Stavka directive (No. 220119) to Govorov at 0215hrs on 21 June reinforced his orders, insisting that the Leningrad Front break through and move on Imatra, Lappeenranta and Virojoki, the aim being to cleanse the Karelian Isthmus of Finnish troops between Viipuri and the Vuoksi River. Govorov had already given Gusev the order to get his 21st Army moving, but he wanted to be sure that he had a truly overwhelming force for the operation, and requested additional troops and equipment from the Stavka. The following day (0200hrs, 22 June) a further directive (No. 220121) informed Govorov that he was not to count on an additional reinforcement of two rifle corps to his Front, as it already had enough forces and the means to complete the task at hand – not an unreasonable response considering the current run of Soviet success on the Karelian Isthmus, coupled with the fact that Operation *Bagration* was due to launch the following day.

Gusev would eventually commit the entirety of his 21st Army – 15 rifle divisions and all supporting artillery and armoured elements – in the attempt to punch through the VKT-Line, but the first stage, launched on the morning of 21 June, consisted of only two rifle corps – Busarov's 97th and Alferov's 109th – attacking the Finnish positions on the western end of the line: The 97th Rifle Corps assaulted towards Haanterä's 3. Prikaati to the west of Lake Kärstilänjärvi while the 109th Rifle Corps attacked to the east of the lake in the direction of Tali and Repola, encountering units from Paalu's 18. Division. Fairly soon it became clear that Finnish resistance had stiffened, and little progress was made until 22 June, when the 97th Rifle Corps forced 3. Prikaati to give some ground and captured Tammisuo, while the 109th Rifle Corps also enjoyed a limited breakthrough, getting to the railway line at Tali. Also on 22 June, the 108th Rifle Corps struck north-west from Viipuri towards Tienhaara on the western side of Suomenvedenpohja Bay, encountering

the freshly arrived JR 61 of Sundman's 17. Division, well-supported with plentiful artillery and rolling air sorties from Gefechtsverband *Kuhlmey* that caused the Soviets no small amount of trouble, blocking their advance in a grinding series of attacks and counter-attacks that saw the attackers fail to win any significant ground.

In comparison with the swift advances and quick triumphs of the preceding days, Gusev's rifle corps enjoyed only a modicum of success in their initial attempts to break through the VKT-Line, unable as they were to extend their small salients into something more significant. The brief check to the Soviet thrust was particularly important for the Finns as it allowed their reinforcements time to arrive in strength, providing some much-needed support to the units manning their stretched and battered front line. The sheer mass of the Soviet attacking forces was what told against the worn-out Finnish units from 4. and 18. divisions in those first days, though the fact that more substantial penetrations had failed to materialize should have been cause for concern among Grusev and his staff, especially considering the paltry standard of Finnish defensive works in the area.

Onni Lindström's regiment (JR 48, led by Colonel Väinö Forsberg) was one of those that had been pushed back by units from the 97th Rifle Corps in the first days of the attack on the VKT-Line. Serving in the 1st Company of Lieutenant-Colonel Sokajärvi's I./JR 48, Lindström recalled how the loss of Viipuri, initially considered unthinkable, had shocked the men of his unit, leaving them with little left to rely upon other than hope and faith. Earlier they had heard endless rumours about the terrible Soviet advance through Kuuterselkä as well as the glory of their own armoured formations in that action. Now, with I. and II./JR 48 digging into a low rocky hill that rose up to the north-east of the village of Konkkala, Lindström experienced the Red Army's war machine at first hand. The furious assault of the Soviet infantry on the afternoon of 24 June very nearly broke through I./JR 48's line, the attack potentially compounded by constant artillery bombardment

A 46-tonne Soviet IS-2 heavy tank makes its way across a bridge. Heavily armoured (up to 100mm for the front of the turret and hull glacis) and sporting a 122mm D-25T gun, the IS-2 was an extremely capable armoured vehicle, though it had a slow rate of fire (2–4rd/min, due to the fact that it used separate ammunition and the cramped state of the turret, which made quick loading difficult). Owing to its limitations of space and the large size of its ammunition it only carried 28 rounds (usually 20 high-explosive and eight armour-piercing shells), and though it was more than a match for any Finnish armoured vehicle, the relative paucity of the latter meant it was more often employed in a direct-fire role against enemy strongpoints and in support of Soviet infantry. (From the fonds of the RGAKFD in Krasnogorsk via Stavka)

and run after run by fighter-bombers, though luckily for the Finns the air and artillery missions were not well-coordinated with the activity of the Soviet infantry, almost entirely missing their targets. The situation was made more miserable by the cold and heavy rain that had begun to fall that afternoon, but which did not seem to hamper the Soviet ground-attack aircraft one bit. The role of JR 48's pioneers proved to be crucial as they had done much work mining all the approaches to Lindström's position, a fact that likely made the difference in the battalion's battle for survival (Lindström 1973: 170–71).

It was clear to Govorov that a more concerted approach would be needed if the Finns were to be broken. On 24 June he ordered Lieutenant-General Simoniak's elite 30th Guard Rifle Corps (the 45th, 63rd and 64th Guards Rifle divisions) to rejoin the 21st Army from its rest positions in the rear area in anticipation of a renewed assault the following day. And so it was that at 0630hrs on 25 June a massive artillery bombardment began to fall along the Finnish line, pounding away for 90 minutes before giving way to massed infantry assaults supported by waves of fighter-bombers. On the Finnish right (west), 3. Prikaati was initially forced back by the 314th and 158th Rifle divisions, but the Finns managed to hold their new position at Lavola against repeated assaults, while the fresh regiments of the 30th Guards Rifle Corps around Tali had more success. Major-General Afanasi Sergeyevich Gryaznov's 110th Rifle Corps was to relieve the divisions of the 109th Rifle Corps, leaving the Guards to take the lead in the renewed attack; Major-General Saveliy Mikhailovich Putilov's 45th Guards Rifle Division promptly achieved a breakthrough to the west of Lake Leitimojärvi, his armoured spearhead racing north-west towards Juustila. To the east of the 45th Guards Rifle Division, Major-General Ivan Danilovich Romantsov's 64th Guards Rifle Division – in conjunction with Colonel Nikolai Dmitrievich Sokolov's 268th Rifle Division (110th Rifle Corps) – broke through along the eastern side of Lake Leitimojärvi, advancing north towards the crucial Portinhoikka crossroads. Nikolay Nikolaevich Inozemtsev, a junior artillery officer who was at Tali on 25 June, remembered how the Soviet artillery-fire missions followed

A Finnish anti-tank gun crew in operation at Ihantala, 30 June 1944. The loader is readying an armour-piercing round for insertion into the breech of a 75 PstK/97-38 anti-tank gun. The weapon was made up from the gun of a French Canon de 75 modèle 1897 (with an added Swiss Solothurn muzzle brake) and mounted on the carriage of the German 5cm PaK 38. It had a rate of fire of 12–14rd/min and its main ammunition consisted of an Armour Piercing Capped Tracer (APC-T) round weighing 6kg and with a velocity of 590m/sec, or a High-Explosive Anti-Tank (HEAT) round weighing 4.6kg and with a velocity of 400m/sec. The APC-T round could penetrate up to 85mm of armour at a 70° angle (70mm at 1,000m, 45mm at 2,500m), while the HEAT round could penetrate 90mm of armour at an angle of 60° at any range. There were 46 75 PstK/97-38 guns in Finnish service, and despite the weapon's fierce recoil it was well regarded, especially as potent anti-tank guns were not available in nearly sufficient numbers, and reliance on the *Panzerfaust* and *Panzerschreck* anti-tank weapons was hampered in the first weeks of the 1944 campaign by poor distribution and inadequate training. (SA-kuva 151075)

on ceaselessly one after the other as he moved to Repola, passing heaps of corpses as well as tanks and guns mired in the mud, dodging Finnish sniper fire all the way (Inozemtsev 2005: 177).

The advance by the 45th and 64th Guards Rifle divisions had developed into a long narrow front nicknamed the *Panssarimakkara* ('tank sausage') by the Finns. It included four Soviet rifle regiments, a tank brigade and several more separate tank and assault-gun regiments, a side-effect of this salient being the need for Forsberg's two battalions of JR 48 to abandon their positions on the rocky hill by Konkkala (Johansen 2016: 286). As the day developed it was clear to the Finns that if the situation was to be saved emergency action was required, so Lagus's Suomen Panssaridivisioona was thrown in to mount a counter-attack on the lead armoured elements of the 45th Guard Rifle Division's advance towards Juustila, taking the Guards battlegroup by surprise and rolling it nearly all the way back to the Soviets' jumping-off point by midnight.

There was little cooperation between Lagus and the headquarters of Paalu's 18. Division, leading to a lack of clear coordination between the defenders at what was a critical period of the battle, but the individual initiative of several Finnish officers proved to be most timely. The best example was provided by Lieutenant-Colonel Reino Inkinen, commander of JR 6 (18. Division). Recognizing the fast-developing threat posed by the 64th Guards Rifle Division's spearhead advancing past the Portinhoikka crossroads, Inkinen scraped together an ad hoc anti-tank force made up of pioneers and assault guns and thwarted any further Soviet advance by 1900hrs, even managing to push them back a little way into the Portinhoikka area, where his force was relieved by Puroma's *Jäger*. Despite the Finnish counter-attacks both Soviet

A Soviet rifle squad with at least two submachine-gunners ready for action. Note that the PPSh-41 SMGs are fitted with the 35-round box magazine as opposed to the more temperamental 71-round drum. A dedicated SMG squad (raised from 1942 onwards) would have 7–8 men, all armed with the PPSh-41 or PPS-43. A rifle regiment's 100-strong SMG company (three platoons, each of three squads) had no heavy weapons of any sort, reflecting its role as the regimental commander's reserve (usually reinforcing scouting parties, or being sent in to support other units in trouble). Within motorized units the SMG companies were often termed *desantnyye tankisty* ('tank-landing troops') and rode into battle on an armoured vehicle's hull and turret; a T-34 was rated to carry eight men, the same number as an SMG squad (Sharp 1995: 103). (Courtesy of the Central Museum of the Armed Forces, Moscow via Stavka)

Guards divisions had made solid breakthroughs, though at a cost – according to the records of the 21st Army its losses for this day alone exceeded 1,000 men. As day turned to night the Finns kept up the pressure, destroying a further 38 Soviet tanks and capturing another seven (which were later added to the Finnish arsenal) before the Suomen Panssaridivisioona's counter-attack came to halt (Nenye 2016: 232). The *Panssarimakkara*, however, remained open.

On the morning of 26 June, Gusev, in anticipation of further Finnish counter-attacks, pushed the as-yet uncommitted 63rd Guards Rifle Division (Major-General Afanasy Fedorovich Scheglov) into the vanguard of his salient in the Finnish line, ahead of the 64th Guards Rifle Division. On the evening of 26 June, Inozemtsev accompanied a brigade commander to the 63rd Guards Rifle Division's temporary headquarters in Aniskala, noting that the night was a stormy one with yet more rain, accompanied by much shelling. More worrying were the small mobile groups of Finnish submachine-gunners that seemed to seep effortlessly through the Soviet front lines, marauding around the rear areas where they cut communication lines, surrounded Soviet units and destroyed ammunition and supply carts. The Soviet losses were heavy (Inozemtsev 2005: 177). Simoniak's 30th Guards Rifle Corps was now fully committed; by the morning of 27 June, the 63rd Guards Rifle Division occupied the area around 3km north-east of the Portinhoikka crossroads, with the 64th Guards Rifle Division to its south-east from Kuusela to Aniskala, and the 45th Guards Rifle Division on the western bank of Lake Leitimojärvi. The 268th Rifle Division (commanded by Colonel Philip Iosifovich Voitulevich, who replaced Sokolov after he was killed by shellfire on 27 June) was at Repola, while Colonel Pyotr Ivanovich Olkhovsky's 168th Rifle Division (also of the 110th Rifle Corps) was to the south-east by Mannikkala.

For the Finns, 26 June brought a little more clarity as the command confusion between the Suomen Panssaridivisioona and 18. Division was eventually resolved, with Lagus given overall field command of both units. A series of Finnish and Soviet counter-attacks clashed on both prongs of the Soviet advance, characterized by several failed Finnish attempts to cut off the *Panssarimakkara* and struggles over the road to Ihantala north of the Portinhoikka crossroads. Paalu's 18. Division, worn out and exhausted from days of near-ceaseless fighting, was withdrawn from the line and replaced by Heiskanen's 11. Division that had arrived to take over the defensive sector stretching between lakes Kärstilänjärvi and Leitimojärvi. The new blood meant that Lagus could pull together his armour and *Jäger* (JR 50 having relieved the latter of their position in the line) for a more concerted and much more ambitious counter-attack on the following day, 27 June.

Lagus aimed to cut off the Soviet spearhead, trapping the 63rd and 64th Guards Rifle divisions in a *motti*, which would then allow the Finns to whittle them down in their usual way. His plan called for the four battalions of Puroma's *Jäger* brigade (supported by a tank company – likely 6. Raskas Panssarikomppania from II./Panssariprikaati which had three platoons, one of two KV-1 'Klimi' heavy tanks, one of four T-28 medium tanks and one

of five T-26 light tanks, when at full strength) to attack the western flank of the Soviet position, aiming for Aniskala and Kuusela. At the same time a task force commanded by Forsberg (I./JR 48, II./JR 48 and III./JR 13, supported by one company from the newly arrived Sturmgeschütz-Brigade 303) was to attack from Ihantala south towards Mutalahti, and Björkman's battlegroup (a detachment of StuG IIIs and a handful of T-26 tanks together with four battalions of infantry from 18. Division) was to strike at Talinmylly and Nurmilampi from the north-east. The simultaneous concentric attacks would be supported by the guns of all the artillery batteries in the area, as well as air support from Finnish Air Force squadrons and elements of Gefechtsverband *Kuhlmey.*

Early in the morning of 27 June the three Finnish attacks crashed into the salient, trying to carve their way through the heavy Soviet defences. All three lines of attack enjoyed some progress, with Puroma's thrust in particular coming close to cutting the Soviet main line of communication, but by the end of the day the Finns on each flank were still 1–2km apart and the two Soviet Guards Rifle divisions remained connected to their Guards Rifle corps. The failure came about in part due to the state of the Finnish troops conducting the attack, all of whom had been engaged in heavy fighting for a number of days. Added to the general level of exhaustion was the fact that the attritional nature of the battle up to this point meant that most of 18. Division and the *Jäger* battalions were unable to muster more than 200 men each for the operation. The Finnish artillery fired around 7,000 rounds in support of the attack, but its effectiveness was somewhat hamstrung by the often very close proximity of the attacking *Jäger* and infantry battalions to the enemy positions, which forced the guns to hold their fire for fear of hitting their own troops.

Inozemtsev's artillery unit was in Aniskala during the Finnish counter-attack, supporting the 64th Guards Rifle Division the headquarters of which was 100m distant through the heavy forest. His unit quickly set up dugouts to avoid the worst of the Finnish artillery fire, the shelling continuing

Ihantala, 13 July 1944: a Finnish soldier aims his MP 40 submachine gun. Only around 150–160 MP 38s and MP 40s arrived in Finland, as crew weapons included with German vehicles such as the StuG III assault gun. The 9×19mm Suomi KP/-31 was the most popular SMG in Finnish service, with a little over 52,600 of them in use by June 1944. Two were issued to each rifle squad, supplemented by captured Soviet SMGs, mostly the PPSh-41 (at least 2,500 captured by the end of the Continuation War) and the PPS-43; a small number of 7.62×25mm PPD-34s, PPD-34/38s and PPD-40 SMGs were also captured, but these tended to be relegated to use by coastal and second-line troops, as were the pre-war 7.65×21mm Bergmann m/20 SMGs of the Finnish police. (SA-kuva 156029)

Jäger attack towards Aniskala

Finnish view: Troops from Jääkäripataljoona 2 ('*Jäger* Battalion 2') assault eastwards towards the Red Army's supply line at Aniskala, moving through the forest and driving into the left flank of the 64th Guards Rifle Division on the morning of 27 June 1944. The attack is part of a combined effort by three Finnish battlegroups to cut off the lion's share of the 30th Guards Rifle Corps, consisting of the 64th and 63rd Guards Rifle divisions. The Soviet corps is leading the push towards Ihantala but has exposed its flanks with the speed of its advance, making it vulnerable to a Finnish counter-attack that, if all goes well, will result in the two leading Guards rifle divisions being trapped in a *motti*.

The other elements of Colonel Puroma's *Jäger* battlegroup – JP 3, JP 4 and JP 5 – are also part of the offensive, attacking on a front to the south of JP 2's position that reaches to the shores of Lake Leitimojärvi. The boldness of the Finnish assault has caught their opponents by surprise, but despite their losses the Soviet troops are fighting back with tenacity, refusing to give ground without a serious fight. The *Jäger* are pushing through the light woods, attacking an ad hoc Soviet position on a forest road; they make the most of cover provided by trees and shell holes, but despite having knocked out one of the defending T-70 light tanks the going is still tough for the Finns.

Soviet view: The lead elements of the Red Army's assault on the VKT-Line had come within a few kilometres of the vital Finnish position at Ihantala when the Finns launched their three-pronged counter-attack on the morning of 27 June. Infantry from the 64th Guards Rifle Division, having borne the brunt of much of the fighting over the past few days, are particularly hard-hit by the unexpected and highly aggressive Finnish attempts to cut the head off the Soviet advance. The *Jäger* have rolled up the first lines of the 64th's defensive screen and are now advancing on a forest road used as a communications route by the 30th Guards Rifle Corps. Two obsolescent T-70 light tanks that were stationed to protect this section of the road have been targeted by multiple *Panzerfaust* shots, knocking out one of them before it could fire more than a few rounds. The remaining tank's commander is firing his 45mm main gun as fast as he can, relying on the surrounding infantrymen to flush out and cut down any remaining Finnish anti-tank teams. The *Gvardeytsy* ('Guardsmen'), remnants of an infantry company that has fallen back on the presumed safety of the armour defending the roadway, are fighting back with determination, none more so than their senior lieutenant; several men are taking cover behind the remaining T-70, while others shelter behind trees or piles of cut logs on the roadside, doing their best to keep the Finns at bay.

through the night of 27/28 June and on into the new day. Finnish artillery shells initially began to drop 80–100m distant, but soon closed to within 25m, forcing Inozemtsev and his gunners into cover, one man marking off each time a new bombardment fell – by the day's end he had counted 22, and the forest that had covered the Soviet gun positions was entirely gone. The crackling of machine-gun fire was proof that the Finns were close by, having slipped along the division's flanks. A telephone wireman, who had gone to repair the line at the command post of a rifle battalion only 2km in front of Inozemtsev's position, did not return – the following morning he was found with a bullet through his temple. On the road from Aniskala to Tali, on which columns of vehicles had travelled freely only the day before, a convoy of 25 trucks filled with ammunition en route to the front line was completely destroyed. The clatter of Finnish machine guns intensified throughout the day, getting closer and closer and forcing Inozemtsev's unit to shelter in their dugouts, hastily screwing fuzes into their stock of hand grenades. The fire became so intense that it was impossible to stand up, with bullets constantly whistling barely a metre above the ground (Inozemtsev 2005: 178).

Despite the failure of his units to cut the head off the Soviet salient, Oesch was keen to keep the pressure on the Soviet line by forming two new attacking groups. To the west, Lagus, with a battlegroup built around elements of the Suomen Panssaridivisioona and supported by JR 30 and I./JR 50, would try to advance along the eastern bank of Lake Leitimojärvi and retake the old Finnish positions at Tali. To the north-east, the leading elements of the arriving Major-General Einar Vihma's 6. Division – JR 6, JR 12, three more infantry battalions and Sturmgeschütz-Brigade 303 – were to move south of Ihantalanjärvi, engaging the Soviet Guards divisions and ideally destroying them. Eino Lohela, a soldier serving in III./JR 12, recalled seeing the worn-out and half-broken men of various Finnish units that his battalion passed on the way to the front, testament to the intensity of fighting that awaited them. He was issued with a *Panzerfaust* and in his first combat with the weapon he was confronted by a mixed armoured column of 28 vehicles, including KV-1 heavy tanks and heavy assault guns (Lohela 1958: 45–46). What Lohela – and the rest of his battalion – had not realized was that their operation was being matched by one of the Soviets' own making.

Ihantala, 13 July 1944: a Finnish soldier prepares his newly acquired 8.8cm Raketenpanzerbüchse 54 or *Panzerschreck* anti-tank rocket launcher. In Finnish service the weapon was known as the 88 rakh/B 54 'Panssarikauhu'; it had an effective range of around 100m and its shaped-charge HEAT warhead was able to punch through 100mm of armour at 60°. The *Panzerschreck* began arriving in Finnish service at the same time as the *Panzerfaust* single-shot anti-tank weapon, and had much the same issues – few Finns knew how to use it in July 1944, meaning much learning had to be done in the field, something that seriously degraded the weapon's potency. (SA-kuva 156037)

A veteran Red Army soldier in a quiet moment. Soviet losses in the first two years of the war were extreme, but by 1943 the Red Army usually dictated the pace of campaigning, allowing it to make better use of its human resources. Many personnel had accrued years of invaluable combat experience that they could now apply to operations that were supported with significant resources and proper planning. Losses could still be significant, but were rarely anything like as consistently bad as those suffered during Operation *Barbarossa*. (Courtesy of the Central Museum of the Armed Forces, Moscow via Stavka)

The Guards rifle divisions had fought hard to retain the integrity of their positions on 27–28 June, but with the brief pause occasioned by the failure of Lagus's armoured counter-attack Gusev opted for another major attempt to break out of the salient. The 63rd Guards Rifle Division struck north, crashing into Forsberg's battlegroup and throwing it back to within 1km of Ihantala; the 268th and 168th Rifle divisions hit out to the north-east, stifling the advance of Björkman's battlegroup; the 64th Guards Rifle Division began to break out to the north-west in a move that threatened to outflank Lagus and Heiskanen's 11. Division; and the 45th Guards Rifle Division attacked to the south of the Portinhoikka crossroads supported by a concurrent thrust northwards by Busarov's 97th Rifle Corps on the division's western flank, threatening to cut off all the Finnish units in the area of Portinhoikka. Despite the best efforts of the Finnish defenders and the heavy toll they were taking on the Soviet rifle divisions and tank regiments, the resources to mount a counter-attack big enough to stop these multiple breaches, let alone throw the Soviet forces back, were non-existent. Shortly after midnight on 29/30 June, Oesch gave the order for all units to pull back to Ihantala and Vakkila where the rest of the newly arrived 6. Division had consolidated new defensive positions, allowing the Finns to shorten their front line.

Reino Lehväslaiho, a *Sotka* (T-34) gunner in the Suomen Panssaridivisioona, was heavily engaged throughout the battle, particularly the hard-fighting days at the end of June. He recalled how all the battalion's tank companies were fully committed, with every day that passed seeing more men and tanks lost forever. Counter-attack after counter-attack, again and again, those still left had to gather their strength so that they could carry out their orders, despite the fact that even the most experienced among them realized that they would likely meet their end in this battle. There were no deserters, however; instead the armoured companies would advance one kilometre and retreat two, fighting on until they were almost insensible, their guns glowing red from use (Nenye 2016: 238). Such strain on men and machines was unsustainable, and they could not be replaced.

In the end, what success the 21st Army enjoyed at Tali–Ihantala owed less to operational manoeuvre than it did to blunt strength, its limited and short-term victories coming through its weight of numbers (both in men and armour) and attrition. Soviet losses for the Leningrad Front – some 67,000 men for the period 10 June to 9 August – though modest in comparison to the horrendous tallies of the Winter War, were hardly insignificant; such casualties were generally not made good by fresh drafts of reinforcements, leading to a gradual degradation of the fighting power of the rifle divisions and their supporting armoured units, with the result that by the end of June their offensive successes were rapidly diminishing. The succeeding weeks would see the various Soviet offensives throughout Finland all run out steam; with no new rifle divisions and tank brigades to replace those that been worn thin by over a month of incessant fighting, a return to the negotiating table now seemed to be an expedient option. For the Finns, simply holding on had proved to be enough. Whatever harsh terms the Soviets were likely to offer, there would be no demand for an unconditional surrender. The Finnish Army had earned that much.

Analysis

SORTAVALA

The Soviet forces facing the Finns were generally well led and reasonably equipped, although much armour and artillery had been drawn away to help with the evolving disaster to the south of Leningrad. Considering the unsuitable Finnish landscape, it is arguable how much value tanks could have added to the Soviet defence, but more artillery would most certainly have been welcome. The troops often gave good accounts of themselves, sometimes extremely so. The systemic shock that was caused by the rapid envelopments by German *Panzergruppen* and which often resulted in whole rifle corps collapsing in a matter of days was not a factor on the Karelian Front. Envelopments did occur – they were a key element of Finnish offensive doctrine – but on more than one occasion the defenders, aided by a variety of often effective field fortifications and stout resistance by the outflanked or encircled infantry, were able to slip the noose, just as the 168th Rifle Division ultimately did at Sortavala. Soviet defensive tactics were designed around narrow defensible fronts that were usually centred on roadways; constricted by their relative lack of mobility, the Soviet forces also relied on mounting constant counter-attacks, usually on a local basis but occasionally on a larger scale, such as that launched by the 198th Motorized Rifle Division, that often helped to blunt Finnish forces' momentum and made their progress much more difficult and costly. It is also notable how, despite being engaged in a month of constant action, the Soviet rifle regiments maintained their cohesion throughout all their reverses and retreats, something that was critical in sustaining an effective defence and ultimately crucial for the success of their eventual escape.

The situation created by Operation *Barbarossa* gave the Finns local superiority in arms and artillery during the attack on Sortavala, an unusual but much-valued factor in the campaign. Finnish tactics, developed before

Finnish tankers relax in front of a captured Soviet T-26 light tank that has been pressed back into Finnish service, East Karelia, 13 October 1941. The Finnish armoured force was to all intents and purposes non-existent during the Winter War, with only 20 obsolete French Renault FT light tanks and six British Vickers Type E Alt B light tanks being available at the time. Post-Winter War adaptations to the Vickers 6-ton design as well as the use of captured Soviet vehicles including T-26s, BT-7 light tanks, and small numbers of T-28 and T-34 medium tanks and KV heavy tanks, allowed the formation of a modest *Panssariprikaati* ('armoured brigade') in early 1942, expanding to a *Panssaridivisioona* ('armoured division') on 30 June 1942. (Ullstein bild/ullstein bild via Getty Images)

the war and refined in 1939–40, were generally successful, and were aided by the nature of the terrain and the Finns' familiarity with operating in it. Breakthrough and pursuit tactics were extensively utilized, as were encirclement tactics and long flanking movements, the Finns sometimes making use of deep 'arrowhead' advances along the roads (Tuunainen 2011: 157). Red Army defences, despite not always being complete, often proved resilient in the face of the best efforts of Finnish gunners, prompting outflanking attacks that forced the Soviets to abandon their strongpoints. More armour or motorized vehicles may have helped the Finns with such rapid advances and envelopments in better terrain, though around Lake Jänisjärvi and Lake Ladoga such opportunities were limited. The *Jäger* battalions, moving with speed (often on bicycles) over dirt tracks and narrow back roads through heavy forest, were the most mobile and flexible of the Finnish formations, but in spite of this capability they mostly found themselves relegated to protecting the eastern flank of the advance.

KUUTERSELKÄ

The start of the Soviet campaign on the Karelian Isthmus was an immediate success, with the two Finnish divisions guarding the border swept aside in a matter of hours, so damaged were they by the power of the Soviet preparatory bombardment. The initial exploitation went smoothly, in part due to the extensive rehearsals that key Soviet units underwent in the months prior to the attack, and the choice of Kuuterselkä as the target of an attempt to break through the VT-Line was a good one, considering its relatively poor defences. The initial attacks went well, with the weak and shallow Finnish line unable to resist for more than a few hours, though local counter-attacks both at Kuuterselkä and against Soviet units attempting to exploit the breakthrough had some limited success. Puroma's more significant counter-attack on the night of 14/15 June was a hastily arranged affair, but it did succeed in pushing the Soviet forces out of the village for a brief period. The impact of Soviet armoured forces at Kuuterselkä, which ought to have been significant due to their numbers and firepower, was somewhat blunted by a combination of difficult terrain and poor coordination at the operational as well as tactical levels, with units tending to behave according to their immediate situation rather than adhering to a more overarching objective (Zaloga 2019: 75). The rifle regiments and artillery support, however, performed creditably. Taken with the overwhelming local superiority that the Soviets marshalled it is unsurprising that the Finns were unable to stem the Red Army's advance.

The Finnish VT-Line at Kuuterselkä was ill-prepared for the weight of armour, air, artillery and manpower that thundered down upon it. In general the VT-Line's state of readiness left much to be desired, especially at Kuuterselkä which relied on a shallow line of infantry bunkers supported by strongpoints and anti-tank obstacles. Defence in depth – well-separated successive lines of strongpoints with interlocking fields of fire for infantry and anti-tank weapons, concentrated on the inevitable chokepoints that would arise in any serious Soviet advance on Viipuri – was not in evidence, the result of unwarranted Finnish apathy and a failure to come to terms with the sort of defensive systems needed to check a Soviet armoured assault. In addition, there was a local shortage of the infantry divisions required to combat such a large attack, with many units positioned in quieter sections of the front while several of those on the Karelian Isthmus were understrength (many of the men having been allowed leave to help with the domestic harvest) and stationed too far back from the front to offer timely support in the early days of the crisis. There was not enough artillery and air power available to IV Corps to degrade Soviet concentrations of force, though this was a systemic issue for the Finns throughout the war. The counter-attack led by Puroma did check the Soviet advance, but only for a day or so at best, and it had no chance of retaking Kuuterselkä with the limited resources at its disposal. A further retreat to the VKT-Line was inevitable.

TALI–IHANTALA

Despite mounting losses of tanks and assault guns, initially the Soviets were able to maintain their armoured forces through regular reinforcement (at least during the first weeks of the campaign), a far cry from the 'bootstrapping' that had characterized their operations in 1941. The Red Army had developed the right machines required to prosecute a deep operation, as well as the systems required to sustain such an operation over weeks or months of attrition. In the Vyborg–Petrozavodsk Offensive this capability was somewhat thwarted by the launch of Operation *Bagration* on 23 June that quickly became the centre

of gravity for Soviet operations, drawing all resources and reinforcements away from the Karelian Isthmus. If the Leningrad Front had achieved all its goals within its given timeframe this would not have been an undue problem, but as the Red Army pushed on past Vyborg the going got much harder, the casualties steeper, the losses in vehicles, artillery pieces and armour more significant. The blunting of Soviet offensive power came about through the stout defence offered by the Finns, but also as a consequence of a lack of cohesion on an operational level within the Red Army's spearheads the deeper they advanced into Finnish territory. The set-piece attacks at the border, much rehearsed and supported by vast artillery and air resources, had been a great success, but by the time Viipuri had fallen there was a noticeable slowing of the pace. Combined-arms operations, though much improved, still lacked consistency, hampered by variable communications, rigid thinking and a lack of initiative.

The shape and character of the Soviet offensive should have been no surprise to the Finns, close observers as they were of the large-scale years-long war raging just to their south, but they failed to develop their defensive capability in two key ways: they neglected to establish defence in depth along the most likely invasion routes to thwart the type of Soviet deep battle operations that had become a feature of the 1943 campaigns in the Ukraine and Byelorussia; and despite the Finns' understanding of the value of anti-tank weapons these were never properly utilized in an integrated system of layered defences. In view of the fact that the Finns had several years to prepare for any Soviet resurgence such failings seem wanton, but two factors should be borne in mind: first, after the 1941 campaign much of the Army was demobilized, with the ongoing border battles of 1942–43 being generally low-intensity affairs that required little in the way of innovation or serious planning; and second, Mannerheim believed that the Red Army would eventually succumb to German military might. Even after Stalingrad and the turning of the tide such a view could be moderated into believing that the Soviets could still be held at bay – it was not until the relief of Leningrad in January 1944 that the likelihood of total German defeat became overwhelming, by which time it was all but too late.

Aftermath

By the end of July 1944, Soviet spearheads on the Karelian Isthmus had been fought to a standstill, the battles of Tali–Ihantala and Vuosalmi blocking any further progress to the south, while by mid-August the battle of Ilomantsi north of Lake Ladoga had thrown back the Red Army's chance to turn the Finnish right flank. The Finns were exhausted but still holding, while the Soviets, their attention now focused on overtaking the fast-retreating German front lines further south, had no more resources – or political interest – to spend in finishing what was for the Stavka essentially a sideshow. So it was that the Continuation War came to a negotiated end with the signing of the Moscow Armistice on 19 September 1944, with Finland battered, hemmed in and now subservient to Soviet foreign-policy machinations, but still free.

The Soviet Union achieved its objective of knocking Finland out of the war, but its victory, much like that won in 1940, was tempered by its high cost and the survival of the Finns as an independent nation. However much Mannerheim wished to think of Finland's 1941 campaign as a separate endeavour from that of the German forces engaged in Operation *Barbarossa*, the success of his undertaking was as reliant upon an overstretched and divided Soviet defence as it was on the calibre and aggression of the Finnish Army. By 1944, when the time came for the Soviets to return, this time in much greater strength and with a battle-hardened army characterized by immensely strong artillery and armoured forces at its core, the Finns again benefited from the fact that for Stalin and the Stavka the main theatre of operations was to be in Byelorussia against the benighted Heeresgruppe Mitte (Army Group Centre). The Soviets certainly had the military might to crush Finland, but in 1944 (as at the end of the Winter War in March 1940) the Finns had made such an endeavour extremely expensive. In 1944's Vyborg–Petrozavodsk Offensive (as in the Winter War) it was good enough for the Soviet Union to render Finland strategically insignificant,

A pair of Finnish infantrymen in front-line trenches at Syskyjärvi, 27 August 1944. The soldier in the foreground wears a Swedish m/26 helmet, while his compatriot sports a German M40. Aside from 34,700 captured Russian m/40 models (20,000 of which were issued to second-line troops), the Finns manufactured 66,893 m/40 helmets during 1940–44 to supplement their pre-war stocks of 80,000 German M16, M17 and M18 helmets. Additional helmets were sourced from Czechoslovakia (the M34, 30,000 purchased in spring 1940), Germany (M35, M35/40 and M35/42 variants, 25,000 in August 1941 and 24,300 in July 1943), Hungary (the m/38, a derivative of the German M35, 75,000 purchased in February 1940), Italy (the m/33, 30,000 bought during 1940–41) and Sweden (8,000 of the m/21 and m/26 models, and a further 20,000 m/37s bought in 1941). (SA-kuva 162224)

though there can be little doubt that if the Finns had been less stubborn or had fought less valiantly the Red Army would have gone on to take Helsinki and everything else besides. It was also to the Finns' advantage that they had kept at least a nominal distance between themselves and their German allies; despite the efforts expended by the Germans on influencing Finnish military planning the Finns, alive to their own needs, politely noted German requests, but made independent decisions that served their own interests best (Tuunainen 2011: 156).

Such independence of mind was on full display in the Lapland War of October 1944–April 1945. One of the terms of the Moscow Armistice (agreed by Finland, the Soviet Union and the United Kingdom on 19 September 1944) demanded that, as well as severing diplomatic links with Germany, the Finns would be responsible for disarming or expelling all German forces remaining in Finland after September 1944. This bloody epilogue saw Finns campaign against their erstwhile allies, helping to drive Generaloberst Lothar Rendulic's 20. Gebirgsarmee (20th Mountain Army) across the border into Nazi-controlled Norway by the end of November 1944.

Finland's three wars resulted in over 295,000 casualties (around 85,000 of them dead or missing) from a population of only 3.7 million people – an extremely high ratio for such a small country to endure. The war's end left Finland poorer financially and with much of its most valuable industrial territory forever lost to its belligerent eastern neighbour, but almost uniquely among the countries of the Baltic and Eastern Europe, it was still a sovereign state. It had earned that right.

UNIT ORGANIZATIONS

Soviet

The M43 (August) rifle division, introduced on 22 August 1943, had 9,380 personnel. A division consisted of a headquarters (NKVD security platoons, reconnaissance and signal companies, anti-tank and two-company engineer battalions), three rifle regiments (2,017 men) and a field-artillery regiment.

A rifle regiment had a headquarters with HQ units (mounted and infantry reconnaissance, engineer and chemical platoons), a signal company, a submachine-gun company (100 men), an anti-tank-rifle company (36 14.5mm anti-tank rifles), medical and supply companies, an anti-tank battery (six 45mm anti-tank guns) and an infantry-gun battery (four 76mm guns), a veterinary hospital, ordnance and transport workshops, and three rifle battalions.

Each rifle battalion had an anti-tank-rifle platoon (nine 14.5mm anti-tank rifles), an anti-tank platoon (two 45mm anti-tank guns), medical and supply platoons, a machine-gun company (nine medium machine guns), a mortar company (nine 82mm mortars), and three rifle companies. A rifle company was composed of a medical section,

a machine-gun section (one medium machine gun) and three rifle platoons, each platoon with three sections of 11 men.

A field-artillery regiment had a headquarters, HQ battery, and three artillery battalions (each with HQ, survey, signal, ammunition and supply platoons). Two of the artillery battalions each had one field-howitzer battery (four 122mm guns) and two field-gun batteries (four 76mm guns each); the remaining artillery battalion had one field-howitzer and one field-gun battery (Thomas 2012: 10).

A Guards rifle division in 1944 (9,680 men) was organized and equipped in much the same fashion as a standard rifle division with the following exceptions. On 22 May 1943 the allotment of submachine guns was increased by 676 (replacing rifles in existing units), bringing the divisional allotment up to 2,426 submachine guns, compared to 1,084 in a standard rifle division. In May 1944 Guards divisions began swapping out their existing anti-tank battalions, each with 12 45mm anti-tank guns, for a self-propelled battalion, each with one T-70 command vehicle and 12 SU-76 self-propelled guns (Sharp 1995: 95).

Finnish

A 1944 infantry division (*divisioona*) consisted of a divisional headquarters, a supply company, two infantry regiments, a field-artillery regiment (three artillery battalions with a total of 36 guns/howitzers), a heavy-artillery battalion (12 guns/howitzers), a heavy-mortar company (120mm mortars), an engineer battalion, a signal battalion, two anti-tank-gun companies (each with six 45–75mm anti-tank guns), a military-police platoon, an anti-aircraft machine-gun company, a field kitchen company and an ambulance platoon.

A 1944 infantry regiment (*Jalkaväkirykmentti*) consisted of a regimental headquarters (a supplies platoon, a *Jäger* platoon, an engineer platoon, a signal platoon and an HQ platoon), a mortar company (6–9 120mm mortars), an anti-tank-gun company (six 45–75mm anti-tank guns), a regimental vehicle column and three infantry battalions.

Each infantry battalion consisted of a headquarters element, a *Jäger* platoon, three infantry companies

(each with a command squad of four men plus three rifle platoons, each rifle platoon containing four squads, each with nine men), a mortar platoon (three 81mm or 82mm mortars), and a machine-gun company (12 Maxim-type machine guns).

A 1944 *Jäger* battalion (*Jääkäripataljoona*) had a headquarters element (a HQ squad, an anti-chemical weapons squad, a signals platoon and a supplies platoon), three *Jäger* companies, a light mortar platoon (1–3 50mm or 81mm mortars), and a machine-gun company (12 m/32–33 Maxims or PM M1910 Maxims). Each *Jäger* company consisted of an HQ squad (11 men), an anti-tank squad (one NCO and eight men armed with two 20mm L-39 anti-tank rifles, one 50mm mortar and from June 1944, often also *Panzerfaust/Panzerschreck* anti-tank weapons), and three or four *Jäger* platoons (each with an HQ element of four men plus four squads, each with nine men).

In 1944 the Suomen Panssaridivisioona consisted of an armoured brigade (*Panssariprikaati*), a *Jäger* brigade (*Jääkäriprikaati*), an armoured anti-aircraft battery (six Landsverk Anti II AA-tanks, 84 men), a heavy-artillery battalion (12 150mm H 40 howitzers), a signals battalion, an engineer battalion, a heavy pontoon platoon, a smoke-camouflage platoon, a replacement battalion and supply units. The 1,131-strong armoured brigade fielded two tank battalions, each with three tank companies equipped with a mix of vehicles, plus a detached tank company, a signal company, an armour school battalion and – from 1944 – an assault-gun battalion (*Rynnäkkötykkipataljoona*), consisting of an HQ company and three assault-gun companies. The *Jäger* brigade consisted of four *Jäger* battalions and an anti-tank battalion (*Panssarijääkäripataljoona*).

BIBLIOGRAPHY

Ahlbäck, Anders (2014). *Manhood and the Making of the Military: Conscription, Military Service and Masculinity in Finland, 1917–39.* Farnham: Ashgate.

Andreyev, Andrey Matveevich (1984). *Ot pervogo mgnoveniya – do poslednego* [*From the First moment to the Last*]. Moscow: Voyenizdat.

Borshchev, Semen Nikolaevich (1973). *Ot Nevy do El'by* [*From the Neva to the Elbe*]. Leningrad: Lenizdat.

Chumak, Ruslan (2011). 'Skol'ko, gde i kogda? O proizvodstve priborov besshumnoy i besplamennoy strel'by «Bramit» v gody Velikoy Otechestvennoy voyny' ['How much, where and when? On the production of "Bramit" silent and flameless firing devices during the Great Patriotic War'], *Kalashnikov Magazine*, 2011, No. 11: 74.

Chumak, Ruslan (2012). 'I snova pro «Bramit» … Novyye svedeniya o razrabotke i proizvodstve priborov «Bramit»' ['And again about the "Bramit" … New information on the development and production of "Bramit" devices'], *Kalashnikov Magazine*, 2012, No. 2: 100.

Chumak, Ruslan (2015). 'Leningradskiye «Bramity». O razrabotke i izgotovlenii priborov dlya besshumnoy i besplamennoy strel'by v blokadnom Leningrade' ['Leningrad "Bramit". On the development and manufacture of devices for silent and flameless firing in besieged Leningrad'], *Kalashnikov Magazine*, 2015, No. 5: 34–36.

Dunn, Walter S. (2009). *Hitler's Nemesis: The Red Army, 1930–45.* Mechanicsburg, PA: Stackpole.

Gritsay, N.T. (1979). 'V boyu — elektrozagrazhdeniya' ['In Battle – Electric barriers'], in Grachev, F.M., *Inzhenernyye voyska goroda-fronta* [*Front-line Engineering Troops*], Leningrad: Lenizdat, pp. 185–88.

Gurkin, V.V. & Lyabin, Yu.Ya. (1958). 'Oboronitel'nyye boi i otkhod 168-y strelkovoy divizii na sortaval'skom napravlenii v iyule – avguste 1941 g.' ['Defensive Battles and Withdrawal of the 168th Infantry Division in the Sortavala Direction in July–August 1941'], in Sychev, K.V. & Malakhov, M.M., *Boyevyye deystviya strelkovoy divizii: Sbornik takticheskikh primerov iz Velikoy Otechestvennoy voyny* [*The Fighting Rifle Division: A Collection of Tactical Examples from World War II*], Moscow: Voyenizdat, pp. 443–466.

Hill, Alexander (2017). *The Red Army and the Second World War.* Cambridge: Cambridge University Press.

Hyvönen, Toivo V. (1975). 'Kuuterselän kujanjuoksu' ['The Gauntlet at Kuuterselkä'], *Kansa Taisteli*, 1975: No. 6: 192–93.

Inozemtsev, Nikolay Nikolaevich (2005). *Frontovoy dnevnik* [*Front Diary*]. Moscow: Nauka.

Johansen, Claes (2016). *Hitler's Nordic Ally? Finland and the Total War 1939–1945.* Barnsley: Pen & Sword Military.

Jowett, Philip & Snodgrass, Brent (2006). *Finland at War 1939–45.* Elite 141. Oxford: Osprey.

Kinnunen, Tiina & Kivimäki, Ville, eds (2012). *Finland in World War II: History, Memory, Interpretations.* Leiden: Brill.

Liimatta, Hannu (2019). *Jalkaväen taktiikan kehittämisen ensimmäiset vuosikymmenet* [*The First Decades of the Development of Finnish Infantry Tactics*]. Helsinki: Suomen Sotahistoriallisen Seuran.

Lindström Onni (1973). 'Juhannusmotti' ['Summer Motti'], *Kansa Taisteli*, 1973, No. 6: 170–71.

Lohela, Eino (1958). 'Keskeytys vihollisen panssarihuollossa' ['Interrupting the Supply of Enemy Armour'], *Kansa Taisteli*, 1958, No. 2: 45–48.

Lunde, Henrik O. (2011). *Finland's War of Choice: The Troubled German–Finnish Alliance in World War II.* Oxford: Casemate.

Mitin, A.M. (1979). 'Sapery 168-y …' ['Sappers of the 168th …'], in Grachev, F.M., *Inzhenernyye voyska goroda-fronta* [*Front-line Engineering Troops*], Leningrad: Lenizdat, pp. 178–82.

Nenye, Vesa, et al. (2016). *Finland at War: The Continuation and Lapland Wars 1941–45.* Oxford: Osprey.

Pipping, Knut, trans. Kekäle, Petri (2008). *Infantry Company as a Society.* Helsinki: National Defence University Department of Behavioural Sciences.

Ponomarev, Yuri (2010). 'Biografiya PBS' ['PBS Biography'], *Kalashnikov Magazine*, 2010, No. 8: 26–30.

Raunio, Ari & Kilin, Juri (2007). *Jatkosodan hyökkäystaisteluja 1941* [*Offensive Battles of the Continuation War 1941*]. Keuruu: Otavan Kirjapaino Oy.

Raunio, Ari & Kilin, Juri (2008). *Jatkosodan torjuntataisteluja 1942–44* [*Defensive Battles of the Continuation War 1942–44*]. Keuruu: Otavan Kirjapaino Oy.

Rautiainen, V. (1962). 'Panssarien kaksintaistelu Kuuterselässä' ['Armour Duel in Kuuterselkä']. *Kansa Taisteli*, 1962, No. 9: 262–66.

Reese, Roger R. (1996). *Stalin's Reluctant Soldiers: A Social History of the Red Army, 1925–1941.* Lawrence, KS: University Press of Kansas.

Rottman, Gordon L. (2010). *World War II Battlefield Communications.* Elite 181. Oxford: Osprey.

Sharp, Charles C. (1995). *'Red Guards': Soviet Guards Rifle and Airborne Units 1941 to 1945.* West Chester, OH: Nafziger Collection.

Thomas, Nigel (2012). *World War II Soviet Armed Forces (3): 1944–45.* Men-at-Arms 469. Oxford: Osprey.

Tillotson, H.M. (1996). *Finland at Peace and War 1918–1993.* Norwich: Michael Russell.

TM 30-430 (1945). *Handbook on USSR Military Forces: Chapter V, Tactics.* Washington, DC: War Department.

Tuunainen, Pasi (2011). 'The Finnish Army at War: Operations and Soldiers, 1939–45', in Kinnunen, Tiina & Kivimäki, Ville, eds, *Finland in World War II: History, Memory, Interpretations*, Leiden: Brill, pp. 139–88.

Vehviläinen, Olli, trans. McAlester, Gerard (2002). *Finland in the Second World War: Between Germany and Russia.* Basingstoke: Palgrave.

Zaloga, Steven J. & Ness, Leland (2009). *Companion to the Red Army.* Stroud: The History Press.

Zaloga, Steven J. (2019). *T-34 vs StuG III: Finland 1944.* Duel 96. Oxford: Osprey.

In one of the better-known images of the Continuation War, Finnish soldiers, possibly from 3. Prikaati ('3rd Brigade', also known as the 'Blue Brigade'), ready themselves before a Soviet attack, 1 June 1942. The informal but distinctive skull motif painted on their helmets was evident earlier in the war in the Uudenmaan rakuunarykmentti ('Uusimma Dragoon Regiment') and 4. Division's KevOs 4 (Kevyt Osasto 4, 'Light Detachment Number 4'). (ullstein bild/ullstein bild via Getty Images)

INDEX